Nov 11, 2020

Calgary

THE HYMNS OF ORPHEUS

Copyright © 2008 BiblioBazaar
All rights reserved

Original copyright: 1792

THE HYMNS OF ORPHEUS

TRANSLATED BY THOMAS TAYLOR

Translated from the Original Greek

With a Preliminary Dissertation on
THE LIFE AND THEOLOGY OF ORPHEUS

THE HYMNS OF ORPHEUS

CONTENTS

PREFACE. 11

A DISSERTATION ON THE LIFE AND THEOLOGY OF ORPHEUS.

SECT. I. 15
SECT. II. 20
SECT. III. 49

THE INITIATIONS OF ORPHEUS.

I.	TO THE GODDESS PROTHYRÆA	63
II.	TO NIGHT.	65
III.	TO HEAVEN.	67
IV.	TO FIRE.	69
V.	TO PROTOGONUS, OR THE FIRST-BORN.	70
VI.	TO THE STARS.	73
VII.	TO THE SUN.	75
VIII.	TO THE MOON	77
IX.	TO NATURE.	80
X.	TO PAN	84
XI.	TO HERCULES.	87
XII.	TO SATURN.	90
XIII.	TO RHEA.	92
XIV.	TO JUPITER.	95

XV.	TO JUNO	96
XVI.	TO NEPTUNE.	98
XVII.	TO PLUTO.	100
XVIII.	TO THUNDRING JOVE	102
XIX.	TO JOVE, AS THE AUTHOR OF LIGHTNING	104
XX.	TO THE CLOUDS.	105
XXI.	TO THE SEA, OR TETHYS	106
XXII.	TO NEREUS.	107
XXIII.	TO THE NEREIDS.	108
XXIV.	TO PROTEUS .	109
XXV.	TO THE EARTH	110
XXVI.	TO THE MOTHER OF THE GODS.	112
XXVII.	TO MERCURY.	114
XXVIII.	TO PROSERPINE.	116
XXIX.	TO BACCHUS.	119
XXX.	TO THE CURETES.	120
XXXI.	TO PALLAS.	121
XXXII.	TO VICTORY.	125
XXXIII.	TO APOLLO.	126
XXXIV.	TO LATONA.	130
XXXV.	TO DIANA.	131
XXXVI.	TO THE TITANS	133
XXXVII.	TO THE CURETES .	134
XXXVIII.	TO CORYBAS	136
XXXIX.	TO CERES.	138
XL.	TO THE CERALIAN MOTHER.	140
XLI.	TO MISES.	141
XLII	TO THE SEASONS.	144
XLIII.	TO SEMELE.	145
XLIV.	TO DIONYSIUS BASSAREUS TRIENNALIS .	146
XLV.	TO LIKNITUS + BACCHUS.	147
XLVI.	TO BACCHUS PERICIONIUS .	148

XLVII.	TO SABASIUS.	149
XLVIII.	TO IPPA	150
XLIX.	TO LYSIUS LENÆUS.	151
L.	TO THE NYMPHS.	152
LI.	TO TRIETERICUS.	154
LII.	TO AMPHIETUS BACCHUS.	156
LIII.	TO SILENUS, SATYRUS, AND THE PRIESTESSES OF BACCHUS.	157
LIV.	TO VENUS.	158
LV.	TO ADONIS.	160
LVI.	TO THE TERRESTRIAL HERMES.	162
LVII.	TO CUPID, OR LOVE.	163
LVIII.	TO THE FATES.	164
LIX.	TO THE GRACES.	166
LX.	TO NEMESIS.	167
LXI.	TO JUSTICE.	169
LXII.	TO EQUITY.	171
LXIII.	TO LAW	172
LXIV.	TO MARS	174
LXV.	TO VULCAN	176
LXVI.	TO ESCULAPIUS.	178
LXVII.	TO HEALTH.	179
LXVIII.	TO THE FURIES	180
LXIX.	TO THE FURIES.	182
LXX.	TO MELINOE.	183
LXXI.	TO FORTUNE.	184
LXXII.	TO THE DÆMON, OR GENIUS.	185
LXXIII.	TO LEUCOTHEA.	186
LXXIV.	TO PALÆMON.	187
LXXV.	TO THE MUSES.	188
LXXVI.	TO MNEMOSYNE, OR THE GODDESS OF MEMORY.	195

LXXVII.	TO AURORA.	197
LXXVIII.	TO THEMIS.	198
LXXIX.	TO THE NORTH WIND.	199
LXXX.	TO THE WEST WIND.	200
LXXXI.	TO THE SOUTH WIND.	201
LXXXII.	TO OCEAN.	202
LXXXIII.	TO VESTA.	203
LXXXIV.	TO SLEEP.	206
LXXXV.	TO THE DIVINITY OF DREAMS.	207
LXXXVI.	TO DEATH.	209

PREFACE.

THERE is doubtless a revolution in the literary, correspondent to that of the natural world. The face of things is continually changing; and the perfect, and perpetual harmony of the universe, subsists by the mutability of its parts. In consequence of this fluctuation, different arts and sciences have flourished at different periods of the world: but the complete circle of human knowledge has I believe, never subsisted at once, in any nation or age. Where accurate and profound researches, into the principles of things have advanced to perfection; there, by a natural consequence, men have neglected the disquisition of particulars: and where sensible particulars have been the general object of pursuit, the science of universals has languished, or sunk into oblivion and contempt.

Thus wisdom, the object of all true philosophy, considered as exploring the causes and principles of things, flourished in high perfection among the Egyptians first, and afterwards in Greece. Polite literature was the pursuit of the Romans; and experimental enquiries, increased without end, and accumulated without order, are the employment of modern philosophy. Hence we may justly conclude, that the age of true philosophy is no more. In consequence of very extended natural discoveries, trade and commerce have increased; while abstract investigations, have necessarily declined: so that modern enquiries, never rise above sense; and every thing is despised, which does not in some respect or other, contribute to the accumulation of wealth; the gratification of childish admiration; or the refinements of corporeal delight. The author of the following translation, therefore, cannot reasonably expect, that his labours will meet with the approbation of the many: since these Hymns are too ancient, and too full of the Greek philosophy, to please the ignorant, and the sordid. However, he hopes they will be acceptable to the few, who have drawn wisdom from its source; and who consider the science of universals, as first in the nature of things, though last in the progressions of human understanding.

The translator has adopted rhyme, not because most agreeable to general taste, but because, be believes it necessary to the poetry of the English language; which requires something as a substitute, for the energetic cadence, of the Greek and Latin Hexameters. Could this be obtained by any other means, he would immediately relinquish his partiality for rhyme, which is certainly when well executed, far more difficult than blank verse, as the following Hymns must evince, in an eminent degree.

And, here it is necessary to observe, with respect to translation, that nothing is more generally mistaken in its nature; or more faulty in its execution. The author of the Letters on Mythology, gives it as his opinion, that it is impossible to translate an ancient author, so as to do justice to his meaning. If he had confined this sentiment, to the beauties of the composition, it would doubtless have been just; but to extend it, to the meaning of an author, is to make truth and opinion, partial and incommunicable. Every person, indeed, acquainted with the learned languages, must be conscious how much the beauty of an ancient author generally suffers by translation, though undertaken by men, who have devoted the greatest part of their lives to the study of words alone. This failure, which has more than any thing contributed to bring the ancients into contempt with the unlearned, can only be ascribed to the want of genius in the translators for the sentiment of Pythagoras is peculiarly applicable to such as these that many carry the Thyrsis, but few are inspired with the spirit of the God. But this observation is remarkably verified, in the translators of the ancient philosophy, whose performances are for the most part without animation; and consequently retain nothing of the fire and spirit of the original. Perhaps, there is but one exception to this remark, and that is Mr. Sydenham: whose success in such an arduous undertaking can only be ascribed to his possessing the philosophical genius, and to his occasionally paraphrasing passages, which would otherwise be senseless and inanimate.

Indeed, where languages differ so much as the ancient and modern, the most perfect method, perhaps, of transferring the philosophy from the one language to the other, is by a faithful and animated paraphrase: faithful, with regard to retaining the sense of the author; and animated, with respect to preserving the fire of the original; calling it forth when latent, and expanding it when condensed. Such a one, will every where endeavour to improve the light, and fathom the depth of his author; to elucidate what is obscure, and to amplify, what in modern language would he unintelligibly concise.

Thus most of the compound epithets of which the following Hymns chiefly consist, though very beautiful in the Greek language; yet when literally translated into ours, lose all their propriety and force. In their native tongue, as in a prolific soil, they diffuse their sweets with full-blown elegance; but shrink like the sensitive plant at the touch of the verbal critic, or the close translator. He who would preserve their philosophical beauties, and exhibit them to others in a different language, must expand their elegance, by the supervening and enlivening rays of the philosophic fire; and, by the powerful breath of genius, scatter abroad their latent but copious sweets.

If some sparks of this celestial fire shall appear to have animated the bosom of the translator, he will consider himself as well rewarded, for his laborious undertaking. The ancient philosophy, has been for many years, the only study of his retired leisure; in which he has found an inexhaustible treasure of intellectual wealth, and a perpetual fountain of wisdom and delight. Presuming that such a pursuit must greatly advantage the present undertaking, and feeling the most sovereign contempt for the sordid drudgery of hired composition, he desires no other reward, if he has succeeded, than the praise of the liberal; and no other defence if he has failed, than the decision of the candid, and discerning few.

A DISSERTATION ON THE LIFE AND THEOLOGY OF ORPHEUS.

SECT. I.

THE great obscurity and uncertainty in which the history of Orpheus is involved, affords very little matter for our information; and even renders that little, inaccurate and precarious. Upon surveying the annals of past ages, it seems that the greatest geniuses, have been subject to this historical darkness as is evident in those great lights of antiquity, Homer and Euclid, whose writings indeed enrich mankind with perpetual stores of knowledge and delight; but whose lives are for the most part concealed in impenetrable oblivion. But this historical uncertainty, is no where so apparent, as in the person of Orpheus; whose name is indeed acknowledged and celebrated by all antiquity (except perhaps Aristotle alone); while scarcely a vestige of his life is to be found amongst the immense ruins of time. For who has ever been able to affirm any thing with certainty, concerning his origin, his age, his parents, his country, and condition? This alone may be depended on, from general assent, that there formerly lived a person named Orpheus, whose father was Œagrus, who lived in Thrace, and who was the son of a king, who was the founder of theology, among the Greeks; the institutor of their life and morals; the first of prophets, and the prince of poets; himself the offspring of a Muse; who taught the Greeks their sacred rites and mysteries, and from whose wisdom, as from a perpetual and abundant fountain, the divine muse of Homer, and the philosophy of Pythagoras, and Plato, flowed;

and, lastly, who by the melody of his lyre, drew rocks, woods, and wild beasts, stopt rivers in their course, and ever, moved the inexorable king of hell; as every page, and all the writings of antiquity sufficiently evince. Since thus much then may be collected from universal testimony, let us, pursue the matter a little farther, by investigating more accurately the history of the original Orpheus; with that of the great men who have, at different periods, flourished under this venerable name.

The first and genuine Orpheus, was a poet of Thrace, and, according to the opinion of many, the disciple of Linus; who flourished, says Suidas, at the time when the kingdom of the Athenians was dissolved. Some assert that he was prior to the Trojan wars, and that he lived eleven, or according to others nine generations. But the Greek word γενεα, or generation, according to Gyraldus, [a], signifies the space of seven years; for unless this is supposed, how is it possible that the period of his life can have any foundation in the nature of things? Plutarch indeed, Heraclitus, Suidas, and some grammarians, assert that this word signifies a space of thirty years: but omitting the discussion of this latter opinion, from its impossibility, we shall embrace the former, agreeable to which Orpheus lived sixty-three years; a period, if we may believe the astrologers fatal to all, and especially to great men, as was the case with Cicero and Aristotle.

Our poet, according to fabulous tradition, was torn in pieces by Ciconian women: on which account, Plutarch affirms the Thracians were accustomed to beat their wives, that they might revenge the death of Orpheus. Hence, in the vision of Herus Pamphilius, in Plato, the soul of Orpheus, being destined to descend into another body, is reported to have chosen rather that of a swan than to be born again of a woman; having conceived such hatred against the sex, on account of his violent death. The cause of his destruction is variously related by authors. Some report that it arose from his being engaged in puerile loves, after the death of Eurydice. Others, that he was destroyed by women intoxicated with wine, because he was the means of men relinquishing their connexion.

Others affirm, according to the tradition of Pausanias, that upon the death of Eurydice, wandering to Aornus, a place in Threspotia, where it was customary to evocate the souls of the dead, having recalled Eurydice to life, and not being able to detain her, he destroyed himself; nightingales building their nests, and bringing forth their young upon his tomb; whose melody, according to report, exceeded every other of this species. Others again ascribe his laceration, to his having celebrated every divinity except Bacchus, which is very improbable, as among the following hymns there are nine to that Deity, under different appellations. Others report that he was delivered by Venus herself, into the hands of the Ciconian women, because his mother Calliope, had not determined justly between Venus and Proserpine, concerning the young Adonis. Many affirm that he was struck by lightning, according to Pausanias; and Diogenes confirms this by the following verses composed as he asserts, by the Muses upon his death:

> Here, by the Muses plac'd, with golden lyre,
> Great Orpheus rests; destroy'd by heav'nly fire.

Again, the sacred mysteries called Threscian, derived their appellation, from our Thracian bard, because he first introduced sacred rites and religion into Greece; and hence the authors of initiation in these mysteries, were called Orpheotelestæ. Besides according to Lucian, our Orpheus brought astrology, and the magical arts into Greece; and with respect to his drawing trees and wild beasts by the melody of his lyre, Palæphatus accounts for it as follows [b]. The mad Bacchanalian nymphs, says he, having violently taken away cattle and other necessaries of life, retired for some days into the mountains. When the citizens having expected their return for a long time, and fearing the worst for their wives and daughters, called Orpheus, and intreated him to invent some method of drawing them from the mountains. But he tuning his lyre, agreeable to the orgies of Bacchus, drew the mad nymphs from their retreats; who descended from the mountains bearing at first ferulæ and branches of every kind of trees. But to the men who were eye-witnesses of these wonders, they appeared at first to bring down the very woods; and from hence gave rise to the fable.

But so great was the reputation of Orpheus, that he was deified by the Greeks; and Philostratus relates, that his head gave oracles in Lesbos, which, when separated from his body by the Thracian women, was, together with his lyre, carried down the river Hebrus into the Sea. In this manner says Lucian [c], singing as it were his funeral oration, to which the chords of his lyre impelled by the winds, gave a responsive harmony, it was brought to Lesbos and buried. But his lyre was suspended in the Temple of Apollo; where it remained for a considerable space of time. Afterwards, when Neanthus, the son of Pittacus the tyrant, found that the lyre drew trees and wild beasts with its harmony, he earnestly desired its possession; and having corrupted the priest privately with money, he took the Orphean lyre, and fixed another similar to it, in the temple. But Neanthus considering that he was not safe in the city in the day time, departed from it by night; having concealed the lyre in his bosom, on which he began to play. But as he was a rude and unlearned youth, he confounded the chords; yet pleasing himself with the sound, and fancying he produced a divine harmony, he considered himself as the blessed successor of Orpheus.

However, in the midst of his transports, the neighbouring dogs, roused by the sound, fell upon the unhappy harper and tore him to pieces. The former part of this fable is thus excellently explained by Proclus in his commentaries (or rather fragments of commentaries) on Plato's Republic; a work I would earnestly recommend to the liberal, for the great light it affords to the recondite theology of the Greeks. Orpheus, says he, on account of his perfect erudition, is reported to have been destroyed in various ways; because, in my opinion, men of that age, participated partially of the Orphic harmony; for they could not receive a universal and perfect science. But the principal part of his melody was received by the Lesbians; and on this account, perhaps, the head of Orpheus, when seperated from his body, is said to have been carried to Lesbos. Fables of this kind, therefore, are related of Orpheus, no otherwise than of Bacchus, of whose mysteries he was the priest. Thus far Proclus, and thus much concerning the first, or Thracian Orpheus. The second Orpheus was an Arcadian, or, according to others, a Ciconian, from Bisaltia of Thrace; and is reported to be more ancient than Homer, and the Trojan war. He composed figments of fables called (μυθοποιΐα) and epigrams; and is, according to Gyraldus, the author of the following hymns; though I rather chuse to refer them, with the Fathers Vossius and Eschenbach, to Onomacritus, or the fourth Orpheus, of Crotonia. The third Orpheus was of Odrysius, a city of Thrace, near the river Hebrus; but Dionysius, in Suidas, denies his existence. The fourth Orpheus was of Crotonia, who flourished in the time of Pisistratus, about the fiftieth Olympiad; and is doubtless the same Onomacritus the author of these hymns. He writ Decennalia, δεκαετηρια, and, in the opinion of Gyraldus, the Argonautics, which are now extant under the name of Orpheus, with other writings called Orphical, but which, according to Cicero [d], some ascribe to Cecrops the Pythagorean. The last Orpheus, was Camarinæus, a most excellent versifier; and the same according to Gyraldus whose descent into hell is so universally known. And thus much for the life of Orpheus.

Footnotes

a   Syntag,. Poet. p. 54.
b   Opusc. Mythol. p. 45
c   In Oratione ad Indoctum.
d   In 1. De Nat. Deor.

SECT. II.

LET us now proceed to his theology; exchanging the obscurity of conjecture for the light of clear evidence; and the intricate labyrinths of fable for the delightful though solitary paths of truth.

And here I must acquaint the reader, that I shall every where deduce my information from the writings of the latter Platonists; as the only sources of genuine knowledge, on this sublime and obsolete enquiry [c]. The vulgar systems of mythology are here entirely useless; and he who should attempt to elucidate the theology, or hymns of Orpheus, by any modern hypothesis, would be as ridiculously employed, as he who should expect to find the origin of a copious stream, by pursuing it to its last and most intricate involutions. In conformity with modern prejudices, the author of the Letters on Mythology, endeavours to prove, that the Orphic hymns deify the various parts of nature, not considered as animated by different intelligences but as various modifications of inert and lifeless matter. This hypothesis is no doubt readily embraced by the present philosophers, a great part of whom, deny the existence of any thing incorporeal; and the better sort, who acknowledge one supreme immaterial Being, exclude the agency of subordinate intelligences in the government of the world; though this doctrine is perfectly philosophical, and at the same time consistent with revelation. The belief indeed of the man, who looks no higher than sense, must be necessarily terminated by appearances. Such a one introduces a dreadful chasm in the universe; and diffuses the deity through the world like an extended substance; divided with every particle of matter, and changed into the infinite varieties of sensible forms. But with the ancient philosopher, the deity is an immense and perpetually exuberant fountain; whose streams originally filled and continually replenish the world with life. Hence the universe contains in its ample bosom all general natures; divinities visible and invisible; the illustrious race of dæmons; the noble army of exalted souls; and men rendered happy by wisdom and virtue. According to this theology, the power of universal soul does not alone diffuse itself to the sea, and become bounded by its circumfluent waters, while the wide expanse of air and æther, is destitute of life and soul; but the celestial spaces are filled with souls, supplying life to the stars, and directing their revolutions in everlasting order. So that the celestial orbs in imitation of intellect, which seeks after nothing external, are wifely agitated in perpetual circuit round the central sun. While some things participate of being alone, others of life, and others are endued with sentient powers; some possess the still higher faculty of reason; and lastly others, are all life and intelligence.

But let us rise a little higher, and contemplate the arguments by which the Platonists, establish the Orphic doctrine of the existence and agency of subordinate intelligences. Thus then they reason [f], Of all beings it is necessary that some should move only, that others should be entirely moved; and that the beings situated between these two, should participate of the extremes, and both move and be moved. Among the first in dignity and order are those natures which move only; the second, those which move themselves; the third, those which move and are moved; and the fourth, those which are moved only. Now the second class of these, or the self-motive natures, since their perfection consists in transition and mutation of life, must depend upon a more ancient cause, which subsists perpetually the same; and whose life is not conversant with the circulations of time, but is constituted in the stable essence of eternity. But it is necessary that the third class, which both move and are moved, should depend on a self-motive nature. For a self-motive being, is the cause of motion to those, which are moved by another, in the same manner as that which is immovable, inserts in all beings the power of moving. And again, that which is moved only, must depend on those natures, which are indeed moved by another, but which are themselves endued with a motive-power. For it is necessary that the chain of beings should be complete; every where connected by proper mediums, and deduced in an orderly and perpetual series, from the principle to the extremes. All bodies therefore belong to those natures which are moved only, and are naturally passive; since they are destitute of all inherent energy, on account of their sluggish nature, which participates of division, magnitude, and weight.

But of incorporeals some are divisible about bodies; while others are entirely free from such an affection about the lowest order of beings. Hence such things, as are divided about the dead weight of bodies, whether they are material qualities or forms, belong to the orders of nature's moving, and at the same time moved. For such as these because incorporeal, participate of a motive faculty; but because they are also divided about bodies, they are on this account exempt from incorporeal perfection; are filled with material inactivity, and require the energy of a self-motive nature. Where then shall we find this self-motive essence? For such things as are extended with magnitude, oppressed by material weight, and inseparably reside in bodies, must necessarily either move only, or be moved by others. But it is requisite, as we have before observed, that prior to this order, the self-motive essence should subsist. And hence we conclude that there is another certain nature exempt from the passivity and imperfection of bodies, existing not only in the heavens, but in the ever-changing elements, from which the motion of bodies is primrily derived. And this nature is no other than soul, from which animals derive their life and motive power; and which even affords an image of self-motion to the unstable order of bodies.

If then the self-motive essence is more ancient than that which is moved by another, but soul is primarily self-motive, hence soul must be more ancient than body; and all corporeal motion must be the progeny of soul, and of her inherent energy. It is necessary, therefore, that the heavens, with all their boundless contents, and their various natural motions (for a circular motion, is natural to such bodies), should be endued with governing souls, essentially more ancient than their revolving bodies. According to the Platonic philosophers, therefore, these souls which orderly distinguish the universe and its contained parts, from their inherent cause of motion, give life and motion to every inanimate body. But it is necessary that every motive essence, should either move all things rationally, or irrationally; that is, either according to the uniform and unerring laws of reason, or according to the brutal impulse of an irrational nature. But the constant order observed in the periods of the celestial bodies, the convenience of positions, and the admirable laws by which their revolutions are directed, plainly evince that their motions are governed by a rational nature. If therefore, an intellectual and rational soul governs the universe, and if every thing eternally moved is under the directing influence of such a soul; may we not enquire whether it possesses this intellectual, perfect, and beneficent power, by participation, or essentially? for if essentially, it is necessary that every soul should be intellectual, since every soul is naturally self-motive. But if by participation, there must be another nature more ancient than soul, which operates entirely from energy; and whose essence is intelligence, on account of that uniform conception of universals, which it essentially contains. Because it is also necessary that the soul, essentially rational, should receive intellect by participation, and that intellectual energy should be of two kinds; one primarily subsisting in the divine intellect; but the other subsisting secondarily in its offspring soul. You may add too, the presence of intellectual illumination in body, which is received in as great perfection as its unstable and obscure nature will admit. For how is it possible that the celestial orbs should be for ever circularly moved in one definite order, preserving the same form, and the same immutable power, unless they participated of an intellectual nature. For soul is indeed the constant supplier of motion; but the cause of perpetual station, of indentity and uniform life, reducing unstable motion to a circular revolution, and to a condition eternally the same, must be more ancient than soul.

Body, indeed, and whatever is the object of sense, belongs; to the order of things moved by another. But soul is self-motive, embracing in itself, in a connected manner, all corporeal motions. And prior to this is immovable intellect. And here it is requisite to observe, that this immaterial nature must not be conceived as similar to any thing inert, destitute of life, and endued with no spirit, but as the principal cause of all motion, and the fountain of all life; as well of that whose streams perpetually return into itself, as of that which subsists in others, and has, on this account only, a secondary and imperfect existence.

All things, therefore, depend upon unity, through the medium of intellect and soul. And intellect is of an uniform essence; but soul of a mental form νοειδήσ, and the body of the world vivific, or vital ζωτικὸς. The first cause of all is indeed prior to intellect, but intellect is the first recipient of a divine nature; and soul is divine, so far as it requires an intellectual medium. But the body which participates a soul of this kind is divine, in as great a degree as the nature of body will admit. For the illustration of intellectual light, pervades from the principle of things, to the extremes; and is not totally obscured, even when it enters the involutions of matter, and is profoundly merged in its dark and flowing receptacle.

Hence we may with reason conclude, that not only the universe, but each of its eternal parts is animated. and endued with intellect, and is in its capacity similar to the universe. For each of these parts, is a universe if compared with the multitude it contains, and to which it is allied. There is, therefore, according to the Orphic and Platonic theology, one soul of the universe; and after this others, which from participating this general soul, dispose the entire parts of the universe into order; and one intellect which is participated by souls, and one supreme God, who comprehends the world in his infinite nature, and a multitude of other divinities, who distribute intellectual essences, together with their dependent souls, and all the parts of the world, and who are the perpetual sources of its order, union, and consent. For it is not reasonable to suppose that every production of nature, should have the power of generating its similar, but that the universe and primary essences should not more abundantly possess an ability of such like procreation; since sterility can only belong to the most abject, and not to the most excellent natures.

In consequence of this reasoning, Orpheus filled all things with Gods, subordinate to the demiurgus of the whole Δημιυργῷ, every one of which performs the office destined to his divinity, by his superiour leader. Hence according to his theology there are two worlds, the intelligible and the sensible. Hence too his three demiurgic principles: Jovial, Dionysiacal, and Adonical, Διι#, (Διι☉) Διονυσιακὴ, Αδωναϊκὴ, from whence many orders and differences of Gods proceed, intelligible [e], intellectual, super-mundane, mundane, celestial, authors of generation. And among these some in the order of guardian, demiurgic, elevating and comprehending Gods; perfecters of works, vivific, immutable, absolute, judicial, purgative, &c. and besides these to each particular divinity, he added a particular multitude of angels, dæmons, and heroes; for according to Proclus, relating the opinion of Orpheus, and the theologists: [f] "About every God there is a kindred multitude of angels, heroes, and dæmons. For every God presides over the form of that multitude which receives the divinity." He likewise considered a difference of sex in these deifies, calling some male, and others female; the reason of which distinction [g] Proclus, with his usual elegance and subtilty, thus explains.

"The division of male and female comprehends in itself, all the plenitudes of divine orders. Since the cause of stable power and identity, and the leader Χὸρηγος of being, and that which invests all things with the first principle of conversion, is comprehended in the masculine order. But that which generates from itself, all various progressions and partitions, measures of life and prolific powers, is contained in the female division. And on this account Timæus also, converting himself to all the Gods, by this division of generated natures, embraces their universal orders. But a division of this kind, is particularly accommodated and proper to the present Theory, because the universe is full of this two-fold kind of Gods. For that we may begin with the extremes, heaven corresponds with earth, in the order and proportion of male to female. Since the motion of the heavens imparts particular properties and powers, to particular things. But on the other hand earth receiving the celestial defluxions, becomes pregnant, and produces plants and animals of every kind. And of the Gods existing in the heavens, some are distinguished by the male division, and others by the female and the authors of generation, since they are themselves destitute of birth, are some of this order and others of that, for the demiurgic choir is abundant in the universe. There are also many canals as it as it were of life, some of which exhibit the male and others the female form. But why should I insist on this particular? since from the absolute unities, whether endued with a masculine, or a feminine form, various orders of beings flow into the universe." Thus far Proclus.

But that Orpheus was a monarchist, as well as a polytheist, is not only evident from the preceding arguments, originally derived from his Theology, but from the following verses quoted by Proclus [h].

> Hence with the universe great Jove contains
> The æther bright, and heav'ns exalted plains
> Th' extended restless sea, and earth renown'd
> Ocean immense, and Tartarus profound;
> Fountains and rivers, and the boundless main,
> With all that nature's ample realms contain,
> And Gods and Goddesses of each degree
> All that is past, and all that e'er shall be,
> Occultly, and in fair connection [i], lies
> In Jove's wide womb, the ruler of the skies.

And in the same place, Proclus has preserved to us another copy of Orphic verses, which are also found in the writer (de Mundo); previous to which he observes, that the demiurgus, or artificer of the world, being full of ideas, comprehended by these all things within himself, as that theologer (Orpheus) declares. With these verses we have connected others, agreeable to the order of Stephens, Eschenbach, and Gesner, as follows.

> Jove is the first and last thund'ring king,
> Middle and head, from Jove all beings spring;
> In Jove the male and female forms combine,
> For Jove's a man, and yet a maid divine;
> Jove the strong basis of the earth contains,
> And the deep splendour of the starry plains;
> Jove is the breath of all; Jove's wondrous frame
> Lives in the rage of ever restless flame;
> Jove is the sea's strong root, the solar light,
> And Jove's the moon, fair regent of the night;
> Jove is a king by no restraint confin'd,
> And all things flow from Jove's prolific mind;
> One is the pow'r divine in all things known,
> And one the ruler absolute alone.
> For in Jove's royal body all things lie,
> Fire, night and day, earth, water and the sky;
> The first begetters pleasing love and mind;
> These in his mighty body, Jove confin'd:
> See, how his beauteous head and aspect bright
> Illumine heav'n, and scatter boundless light!
> Round which his pendant golden tresses shine
> Form'd from the starry beams, with light divine;
> On either side two radiant horns behold,
> Shap'd like a bull's and bright with glittering gold;
> And East and West in opposition lie,
> The lucid paths of all the Gods on high;
> His eyes, the sun, and moon with borrow'd ray;

Royal, ætherial; and his ear refin'd
Hears ev'ry voice, and sounds of ev'ry kind.
Thus are his head and mind immortal, bright,
His body's boundless, stable, full of light;
Strong are his members, with a force endu'd
Pow'rful to tame, but ne'er to be subdu'd;
Th' extended region of surrounding air
Forms his broad shoulders, back, and bosom fair;
And thro' the world the ruler of the skies
Upborne on natal, rapid pinions flies;
His sacred belly earth with fertile plains,
And mountains swelling to the clouds, contains;
His middle zone's the spreading sea profound,
Whose roaring waves the solid globe surround;
The distant realms of Tartarus obscure
Within earth's roots, his holy feet secure;
For these earth's utmost bounds to Jove belong,
And form his basis permanent and strong.
Thus all things Jove within his breast conceal'd,
And into beauteous light from thence reveal'd.

These verses contain what Dr. Cudworth calls the grand arcanum of the Orphic theology, that God is all things; which is likewise an Egyptian doctrine, from whence it was derived through Orpheus into Greece: and this sublime truth Plotinus [1] himself proves with his usual sagacity and depth. But here it is necessary to observe, that Orpheus and the Platonists do not conceive the Deity to be all things, as if he were a divisible, corporeal nature; but that he is all things, because present every where, and to every being totally, though more or less intimately present, according to the various gradations and approximations of being. So that he is to be considered as containing all things, and yet as separate and apart from all; as the source of all multitude, yet himself perfect unity; and as immensly prolific, yet divinely solitary and ineffably good. Thus, according to Porphyry [m], explaining the properties of incorporeal natures, God, intellect, and soul are each of them every where, because no where. But God is every where, and at the same time, in no place of any being posterior to his nature; but he is only such as he is, and such as he willed himself to be. But intellect is indeed in the Deity, yet every and in no place of its subordinate essences. And soul is in intellect, and in the Deity, every where and no where with respect to body; but body exists in and in intellect, and in God. And though all beings, and nonentities, proceed from, and subsist in the Deity, yet he is neither entities, or nonentities, nor has any subsistence in them. For if he was alone every where, he would indeed be all things, and in all: but because he is likewise no where, all things are produced by him; so that they subsist in him because he is every where, but are different from him because he is no where. Thus also intellect being every where and no where, is the cause of souls, and of natures subordinate to soul: at the same time it is neither soul, nor such things as are posterior to the soul, nor has it any subsistence in them; and this because it is not only every where in its subordinate natures, but at the same time no where. Thus too, soul is neither body, nor in body, but is the cause of body; because while it is every where diffused through body, it is no where. And this procession of the universe, extends as far as to that nature [n], which is incapable of being at the same time every where and no where, but which partially participates of each, And in another place of the same excellent fragment, he tells us that the ancients explaining the property of an incorporeal nature, as far as this can be effected by discourse, when they affirmed it to be one, at the same time add, that it is likewise all things; that it is every where, and no where, and that it is totally present in every whole. He adds, they express its nature entirely by contrary properties, that they may remove from it the fictitious and delusive conceptions of bodies which obscure those properties by which true being is known.

We have before observed, that the Platonic philosophers, agreeable to the doctrine of Orpheus, considered fecundity as, in an eminent degree, the propery of a divine nature; and from this principle filled the universe with Gods P. This opinion a modern philosopher, or a modern writer on mythology, will doubtless consider as too ridiculous to need a serious refutation the one, because he believes the phenomena may be solved by mechanical causes; and the other, in consequence of a system originating from prejudice, and supported without proof. However, prejudice apart, let us hear what the philosophers can urge in defence of this doctrine, in addition to what we have already advanced. To begin then with Onatus q the Pythagorean: "Those," says he, "who assert that there is but one God, and not many Gods, are deceived, as not considering that the supreme dignity of the divine transcendency consists in governing beings similar to itself, and in surpassing others. But the other Gods have the same relation to this first and intelligible God, as the dancer, to the Coryphæus, and as soldiers to their general, whose duty is to follow their leader. And although the same employment is common both to the ruler, and those who are ruled; yet the latter, if destitute of a leader, could no longer conspire together in one occupation; as the concord of the fingers and ` dancers, and the expedition of the army, must fail, if the one is deprived of the Coryphæus and the other of the captain or commander." To the same purpose Plotinus r shews that it is perfectly philosophical to suppose a multitude of Gods subordinate to the One supreme. "It is necessary," says he, "that every man should endeavour to be as good as possible, but at the same time, he should not consider himself as the only thing that is good but should be convinced that there are other good men, and good dæmons in the universe, but much more Gods: who though inhabiting this inferior region, yet look up to that higher world; and especially that most blessed Soul, the ruling Divinity of this universe. From whence a man ought to ascend still higher, and to celebrate the intelligible Gods, but above all their great King; declaring his majesty in a particular manner, by the multitude of Gods subordinate to his divinity. For it is not the province of those who know the power of God, to contract all into one, but rather to exhibit all that divinity which he has displayed, who himself, remaining one, produces many, which proceed from him and by him. For the universe subsists by him, and perpetually speculates his divinity, together with each of the Gods it contains." Should it be objected, that if such Gods (or exalted beings) really existed, we should be able to demonstrate the reality of their existence, in the same manner as that of one supreme God; we cannot frame a better reply than in the words of Proclus [s]. "And perhaps," says he, "you may affirm that souls more swiftly forget things nearer to them; but have a stronger remembrance of superior principles. For these last operate on them more vigorously, through the sublimity of their power, and appear to be present with them by their energy. And this happens with respect to our corporeal fight; which does not perceive many things situated on the earth, yet observes the inerratic sphere, and the stars it contains; because these strongly irradiate our eyes with their light. So the eye of our soul is more forgetful, and sooner loses the sight of principles proximate to its nature, than of such as are more elevated and divine. In like manner all religions and sects confess that there is one highest principle, and men every where invoke God as their helper; but that there are Gods in subordination to this first cause, and that there is a providence proceeding from these to the universe, all men do not believe; and this because the one appears to them more perspicuously than the many."

Indeed in consequence of the Platonic doctrine of the pre-existence of the soul, it is not strange that we should know so little of those divine and exalted beings above us; since from our union with generation and material concerns, we are imbued with oblivion, ignorance, and error. "We are similar," as Porphyry [t] well observes, "to those who enter or depart from a foreign region, not only in casting aside our native manners and customs; but from the long use of a strange country we are imbued with affections, manners, and laws foreign from our natural and true religion, and with a strong propensity to these unnatural habits." As, therefore, it is not wonderful that the greatest part of those who inhabit a pestiferous region, should languish and decline, but that a very few should preserve their natural strength; so we ought not to wonder, that thus placed in generation, the multitude of mankind are obnoxious to passions and depraved habits; but we ought rather to be astonished if any souls, thus involved in the dark folds of the body, and surrounded with such great and unceasing mutations, are found sober, pure, and free from destructive perturbations. For it is surely astonishing that the soul should live immaterially, in material concerns; and preserve itself uncontaminated amidst such base defilements; that it should drink of the cup of oblivion, and not be laid asleep by the intoxicating draught; that it should elevate its eye above the sordid darkness with which it is surrounded; and be able to open the gates of truth, which, though contained in its essence, are guarded and shut by terrene and material species. But that it is possible to know more of such exalted natures than is generally believed, by the assistance of the ancient philosophy, accompanied with a suitable life, is, I am persuaded, true; and I would recommend the arduous and glorious investigation to every liberal mind.

Let us now consider the nature of sacrifice according to Orpheus and the Platonists; previous to which, I must beg leave to inform the reader, that the Greek theologists and philosophers were not (as they are represented by modern writers on mythology) so stupid as to worship the creature instead of the Creator; and to neglect or confound that homage and veneration, which is due to the first cause of all. On the contrary, they considered the supreme Being as honoured by the reverence paid to his most illustrious offspring; and carefully distinguished between the worship proper to the Deity, and to the subordinate Gods, as the following discourse will abundantly evince. How, far indeed, such opinions maybe consistent with revelation, it is not my business to determine. It is sufficient for me, to give the most faithful account I am able of their sentiments on this subject; to free their opinions from misrepresentation; and to shew that God has not left himself without a witness among the wise and learned of the heathens. But as I cannot give a better account of the nature and antiquity of sacrifice than from the writings of Porphyry, I shall present the reader with the following paraphrase, on part of the second book of his excellent work on abstinence.

"The period of time appears to have been immensely distant, from which, as Theophrastus says, a nation the most learned of all others, and inhabiting the sacred region formed by the Nile, began first of all, from the domestic fire, to sacrifice to the celestial divinities; not with myrrh or cassia, nor with the first fruits of frankincense mingled with saffron, (for these were applied many ages afterwards, from error increasing in certain degrees: I mean at the period when men having surmounted the difficulties of a life, formerly oppressed with the cares of procuring necessaries, and from the beginning to the end attended with many labours and tears, sacrificed perhaps a few drops to the Gods.) For at first they performed sacrifices, not with aromatics but with the first fruits of the green herb; plucking it with their hands, as a certain soft down or moss of prolific nature. Indeed the earth produced trees before animals; but prior to trees, the annually rising grass, the leaves, and roots, and entire produce of which having collected, they sacrificed with fire: by this sacrifice, saluting the visible celestial Gods, and rendering them through the ministry of fire immortal honours. For we preserve as sacred to those divinities, a perpetual fire in our temples; since this element is most similar to their lucid frames. But with respect to fumigations from herbs produced by the earth, they called the censer or pan, in which the herbs were burnt, θυμιατήριος, and to perform sacrifice θύειν, and the sacrifices themselves θυσίαι all which we have erroneously interpreted, as if these words were signatures of that error, which afterwards crept in among us; and hence it is that we call the worship consisting from the slaughter of animals θυσίαι.

Indeed so great was the care of the ancients, in retaining their pirmæval customs, that they uttered imprecations against those who deserted the old manner, and introduced a new one: and therefore they called those herbs with which we now fumigate αρωμάτα, aromatics. But the antiquity of the above mentioned fumigations will be perceived by him who considers that even now many odorous kinds of wood, cut into fragments, are employed in sacrifice. From whence it happened that the earth now bearing trees together with grass, its earliest production, men at first eating the fruits of oaks, burned only a few of these in sacrifices to the Gods, on account of the rarity of such sustenance; but sacrificed a multitude of the leaves. Afterwards human life passed to a gentle diet, and sacrifices were performed with nuts; from whence the proverb originated, ἅλις δρυός, enough of the oak.

"But among the fruits of Ceres, after the first appearance of leguminous barley, mankind were accustomed to sprinkle it, made into an entire mass, in their first sacrifices. Afterwards breaking the barley, and diminishing the nutriment into meal, having concealed the instruments of so great a work, which afford divine assistance to human life, they approached these as certain sacred concerns. But they cast the first fruits of the barley (when bruised into meal) and which was more esteemed than when whole, into the fire, in sacrifice to the Gods: from whence even now, at the conclusion of the sacrifice, we make use of meal mixed with wine and oil. By this custom indeed we indicate from whence, and from what beginnings sacrifices have increased to the present state: but, at the same time, we do not consider why such things are performed. Mankind proceeding from these small beginnings, and the earth yielding an abundant supply of corn and various fruits, they judged that the first produce of all the rest should be offered in sacrifices, with a view of pleasing the various orders of the Gods: selecting many things for this purpose, and mingling not a few others with these, if they possessed any thing beautiful, and on account of its odoriferous nature accommodated to divine sensation. With some of these, formed into garlands, they encircled the statues of the Gods; and others they sacrificed with fire. Likewise to the Gods as the proper causes, they poured forth the divine drops of wine, and honey, and oil, when their uses were first discovered.

"The truth of the preceding account appears to be confirmed by the procession celebrated even now at Athens, in honour of the sun and the hours. For in this solemnity grass is carried about, enwrapping the kernels of olives, attended with figs, all kinds of pulse, oaken boughs or acorns, the fruit of the strawberry, wheat, and barley, a mass of dried figs, cakes composed from the meal of wheat and barley, heaped in a pyramidal form, and last of all olives." Theophrastus then proceeds to shew the impropriety of animal sacrifices, after which he adds: "But the utility of fruits is the first and greatest of every production; the first fruits of which are to be sacrificed to the Gods alone, and to the Earth, the prolific parent of every herb.

For Earth is the common Vesta of Gods and men, on whose fertile surface reclining, as on the soft bosom of a mother or a nurse, we ought to celebrate her divinity with hymns, and incline to her with filial affection, as to the source of our existence. For thus, when we approach to the conclusion of our mortal life, we shall be thought worthy of a reception into the celestial regions, and of an association with the race of immortal Gods, who now behold us venerating their divinities with those fruits, of which they are the authors, and sacrificing in their honour every herb of the all-bearing earth; at the same time not esteeming every thing worthy or proper to be offered as a testimony of our homage. "For as everything indiscriminately is not to be sacrificed to the Gods, so perhaps we cannot find any thing sufficiently worthy, with which we may worship them as they deserve." Thus far Theophrastus. Porphyry then proceeds to shew after what manner those ought to sacrifice who propose an intellectual life, as the ultimate object of their pursuit.

"Let us also," says be, "sacrifice, but in a manner becoming the offspring of intellect, bringing with us the most exalted offerings, with our most exalted powers. To the Divinity indeed, who is above all things, as a wise man said, neither sacrificing nor dedicating any thing sensible or material; for there is nothing subsisting by material concretion, which must not be deemed impure by a nature entirely free from the contagion of body. Hence even the discourse, which is proffered by the voice is not proper to be addressed to a cause so sublime and ineffable; nor the internal speech of the soul, if contaminated with any perturbation, or mixed with any of the sensible phantasms of imagination. But we ought to worship the supreme God, in the most profound and pure silence; and with the purest thoughts concerning his exalted nature. It is requisite, therefore, that having conjoined and assimilated ourselves to him, we should approach this sublime principle with a pious sacrifice, which may redound to his praise, and to our safety. But such a sacrifice can only be performed by contemplating his divinity with a soul free from material affections, and with the rational eye filled with intellectual light. But to the offspring of this first God (I mean the intelligible divinities) we should present the sacrifice of hymns, composed by the rational principle. For it is customary to offer the first-fruits of such things as every, God bestows upon us; by which he nourishes and supports our existence, and which are subservient to the purposes of sacrifice. As the husbandman, therefore, performs sacred rites, by presenting handfuls of pulse and fruits, so ought we to sacrifice our purest thoughts, and other goods of the soul, thanking the divinities for the sublime contemplations they afford us, and for truly feeding our intellectual part with the speculation of their essences; for, conversing with us, and appearing to our mental sight; for shining upon us with divine splendours, and by this means procuring for us true salvation.

"But an exercise of this kind is performed in an indolent manner, by many who apply themselves to philosophy, and who more sedulously cultivating fame than honouring the divinity, are wholly employed about statues, taking no care to learn after what manner, or whether or not these intellectual beings are to be adored; nor by properly consulting divine concerns, are they anxious to know, in how great a degree, we ought to strive after an union with these exalted natures. With such as these we by no means contend; since our only endeavour is to obtain a knowledge of divinity, and to imitate pious and ancient men, by frequently sacrificing of that contemplation which the Gods have bestowed upon us, and by the use of which we are partakers of real salvation.

"The Pythagoreans indeed who were very studious of numbers and lines, for the most part sacrificed of these to the Gods; denominating this number Minerva [c], another Apollo; and again, this justice, and another Temperance. They proceeded also in a similar manner in geometrical figures. Hence they pleased the divinities by sacrifices of this kind, calling each of them by their proper names, for the purpose of obtaining their particular requests. They often besides made such invocations subservient to the purposes of divination; and if they required the investigation of any thing particular, they used the visible celestial Gods, also the wandering and fixed stars, of all which the sun ought to be placed as a leader, next to this the moon; and, as a theologian observes, we should make fire allied to these by a proximate conjunction. But the same person asserts that the Pythagoreans sacrificed no animal, but offered the first fruits of flour and honey, and of the diversified productions of the earth; nor kindled fire on the bloody altar, says he, with other things of a similar nature: but why should I transcribe such relations? For he who is truly studious of piety, knows why he ought not to sacrifice any thing animated to Gods; but alone to genii, and other powers superior to man, whether good or bad: he likewise knows to what kind of men it belongs to sacrifice these, and every circumstance respecting those beings, who require such sacrifices to be performed. With regard to other particulars I shall be silent. But what some Platonists have divulged will perspicuously illustrate the subject before us, which I shall relate as follows.

"The first God, since he is incorporeal, immoveable, and indivisible, neither existing, in any being, place, or time, nor even circumscribed by, and as it were invested with himself, is in no respect indigent of any thing external to his nature, as we have already observed. But this last property of a divine essence is likewise true of the soul of the world, possessing a triple divisibility, and being naturally self-motive, yet so constituted that it chuses to move in an orderly and beautiful manner, and to agitate the corporeal fabric of the world according to the most excellent and harmonious reasons. But it associates to itself and is circularly invested with body, although incorporeal and entirely destitute of passion. But to the other Gods, to the world, and to the erratic and fixed stars, composed from body and soul, and to the visible divinities, testimonials of gratitude are to be offered by sacrificing with inanimate substances. After these there remains that multiude of invisible beings, which Plato indiscriminately calls dæmons. Some of these are allotted a peculiar name by mankind, from whom they obtain divine honours and other kinds of religious worship: but others of these are for the most part called by no peculiar name, but are obscurely worshipped by some men, and are denominated according to certain streets or cities. But the remaining multitude are called by the common name of dæmons. Concerning all these, a general persuasion obtains, that their influence is noxious and malignant if they are once angered because their accustomed worship is neglected; and that they are again benificent if appeased by prayers and supplications, by sacrifices and convenient rites.

"But the confused opinion which subsists concerning these beings, and which has proceeded to great infamy, requires that we should distinguish their nature according to the decisions of reason. After this manner then they are distributed. As many souls as proceeding from the universal soul, administer considerable parts of those places contained under the lunar orb, who are indeed connected with an aerial part, but subject it to the dominion of reason, are to be esteemed good dæmons. We ought to believe that all their operations tend to the utility of the concerns subject to their dominion, whether they preside over certain animals, or over fruits assigned to their charge, or over things subservient to these particulars; such as prolific showers, moderate winds, serene weather, and whatever is calculated to promote these, as a good temperament of the seasons of the year, &c. They likewise administer to us the use of music, and of every discipline, together with the medicinal and gymnastic arts, and whatever else is allied to these. For it is impossible that such dæmons can supply what is convenient and proper; and at the same time be the authors of things destructive and improper. In this class the messengers, as Plato calls them, between Gods and men must be numbered, who convey our prayers and pious offerings to the Gods as judges of our conduct, and bring back to us in return divine warnings, exhortations, and oracles. But as many souls as do not properly govern the aerial part with which they are connected, but are for the most part subdued by its influence, and are agitated and hurried away by its brutal power in a rash and disorderly manner, whenever the wrathful irritations and desires of the pneumatic part grow strong; souls of this kind are properly denominated dæmons, but ought at the same time to be called malevolent and base.

"All these, together with those who obtain a contrary power, are invisible, and entirely imperceptible to human sensation for they are not invested like terrene animals with a solid body; nor are they all endued with one shape; but they possess a diversity of forms. However, the forms impressed on their aerial part, are sometimes apparent, and at other times obscured. Sometimes too evil dæmons change their shapes. But this pneumatic part, so far as corporeal, is subject to passion and change; and although it is so confined by the coercive power of these demoniacal souls, that its form continues for a long time, yet it is not by this means eternal. For is reasonable to believe, that something continually flows from this aerial part; and that it receives a nutriment accommodated to its nature. Indeed the πνευμα, or aerial part of the good dæmons, consists in a certain commensurate proportion, in the same manner as those bodies which are the objects of our present perception. But the bodies of the malevolent dæmons are of a discordant temperament, on which account they inhabit that aerial space proximate to the earth, with a passive affection; and for the most part govern things subject to their dominion with a turbulent malignity. Hence there is no evil which they do not endeavour to perpetrate. For their manners are entirely violent and fraudulent, and destitute of the guardian preservation of better dæmons; so that they machinate vehement and sudden snares with which they rush on the unwary; sometimes endeavouring to conceal their incursions, and sometimes acting, with open violence against the subjects of their oppression." Thus far Porphyry: the length of which quotation needs no apology; both on account of its excellence, and because the unlearned reader will not find it elsewhere in English. I would also add that I wish (with a proper sense of the greatness of the undertaking) to offer this, together with the preceding and subsequent paraphrases, as specimens of that method mentioned in the Preface to this Work; and which I cannot but consider as the best means of exhibiting the Greek philosophy in modern languages.

Having then discoursed so largely from Porphyry concerning sacrifice, and as he particularly recommends the sacrifice performed by contemplation and divine hymns; let us hear his sentiments concerning the nature of prayer, as they are preserved to us by Proclus in his excellent Commentary on the Timæus, p. 64. "It is requisite (says Proclus) before all things, that we understand something perspicuously concerning the nature of prayer: I mean in what its essence consists, what its perfection is, and from whence it becomes natural to our souls. He then proceeds to relate the opinion of Porphyry as follows. For Porphyry discoursing concerning such of the ancients as either approved of, or exploded prayer, leads us through various opinions, which I shall now summarily relate. Neither those who labour under the first kind of impiety, I mean denying the existence of the Gods, claim any advantage to themselves from prayer: nor yet those of the second class, who entirely subvert a providence; for though they acknowledge the existence of the Gods, yet they deny their provident concern for the affairs of the universe. Nor again those of a third order, who they confess that there are Gods, and that their providence extends to the world, yet consider all things as produced by the divinities from necessity: for the utility of prayer is derived from such things as are contingent, and may have a different existence. But those who both acknowledge the being of the Gods, and their continual providence, and that some events are contingent, and may subsist in a different manner; these men indeed may be truly said to approve of prayer, and to confess that the Gods correct our life, and establish it in safety. Proclus then proceeds to relate the reasons by which Porphyry confirms its utility. "He adds that prayer in a particular manner pertains to worthy men, because it conjoins them with divinity; for similars love to be united together: but a worthy man is in an eminent degree similar to the divine natures. We may likewise add, that since good men are placed in custody, and confined by the dark bands of the body as in a prison, they ought to pray to the Gods, that it may be lawful for them to depart from hence. Besides, since we are as children torn from the bosom of our parent, we ought on this account to request by our prayers that we may return to the Gods our true intellectual parents. If this is the case, do not they who deny that prayers are to be offered to the Gods, and who prevent their souls from being united with the divinities, that is with beings more excellent than themselves, appear similar to those who are deprived of their parents? Lastly, all nations who have flourished in the exercise of wisdom, have applied themselves to divine prayers: as the Bramins among the Indians, the Magi among the Persians, and amongst the Greeks also, those who have excelled in the science of theology: for on this account they instituted mysteries and initiatory rites (τελεται). Besides, this consideration is not to be omitted, that since we are a part of this universe, it is consonant to reason that we should be dependent on it for support. For a conversion to the universe procures safety to every thing which it contains. If therefore you possess virtue, it is requisite you should invoke that divinity which previously comprehended in himself every virtue: for universal good is the cause of that good which belongs to you by participation. And if you seek after some corporeal good, the world is endued with a power which contains universal body. From hence therefore it is necessary that perfection should also extend to the parts. Thus far that most excellent philosopher Porphyry; in which quotation, as well as the preceding, the reader must doubtless confess, that Proclus did not without reason admire him, for what he calls his τὰ ἱεροπρεπῆ νοήματα, or conceptions adapted to holy concerns; for surely no philosopher ever possessed them in a more eminent degree.

If it should be asked, in what the power of prayer consists, according to these philosophers? I answer, in a certain sympathy and similitude of natures to each other: just as in an extended chord, where when the lowest part is moved, the highest presently after gives a responsive motion. Or as in the firings of a musical instrument, attempered to the same harmony; one chord trembling from the pulsation of another. as if it were endued with sensation from symphony. So in the universe, there is one harmony though composed from contraries; since they are at the same time similar and allied to each other. For from the soul of the world, like an immortal self-motive lyre, life every where resounds, but in some things more inferior and remote from perfection than in others. And with respect to the super-mundane Gods, sympathy and similitude subsists in these as in their most perfect exemplars; from whence they are participated by sensible natures, their obscure and imperfect images. Hence (say they) we must not conceive, that our prayers cause any animadversion in the Gods, or, properly speaking, draw down their beneficence; but that they are rather the means of elevating the soul to these divinities, and disposing it for the reception of their supernal illumination. For the divine irradiation, which takes place in prayer, shines and energizes spontaneously, restoring unity to the soul, and causing our energy to become one with divine energy. For such, according to these philosophers, is the efficacy of prayer, that it unites all inferior with all superior beings. Since, as the great Theodorus says, all things pray except the first.

Indeed so great is the power of similitude, that through its unifying nature all things coalesce, and impart their particular properties to ethers. Whilst primary natures distribute their gifts to such as are secondary, by an abundant illumination, and effects are established in the causes from which they proceed. But the connection and indissoluble society of active universals, and of passive particulars, is every where beheld. For the generative causes of things, are contained by similitude in their effects;

and in causes themselves their progeny subsist, comprehended in perfect union and consent. Hence the celestial orbs impart a copious defluxion of good to this terrestrial region; while sublunary parts, assimilated in a certain respect to the heavens, participate a perfection convenient to their nature.

Hence too, from the progressions of similitude, there are various leaders in the universe. And many orders of angels dancing harmoniously round their ruling deities; together with a multitude of dæmons, heroes, and particular souls. There are besides multiform kinds of mortal animals, and various powers of plants. So that all things tend to their respective leaders, and are as it were stamped with one sign of domestic unity; which is in form more evident., and in others more obscure. For indeed similitude in first productions subsists more apparently; but in those of the middle and extreme orders is obscured in consequence of the gradations of progression. Hence images and exemplars derive their hypostasis from conciliating similitude; and every thing through this is familiar to itself, and to its kindred natures.

But it is time to return from this digression to the business of sacrifice and prayer. That we may therefore have a clearer view of the nature and efficacy of each, let us hear the elegant and subtle Proclus [x], upon sacrifice and magic, of which the following is a paraphrase.

"In the same manner as lovers gradually advance from that beauty which is apparent in sensible forms, to that which is divine; so the ancient priests, when they considered that there was a certain alliance and sympathy in natural things to each other, and of things manifest to occult powers, and by this means discovered that all things subsist in all, they fabricated a sacred science, from this mutual sympathy and similarity. Thus they recognized things supreme, in such as are subordinate, and the subordinate in the supreme: in the celestial regions terrene properties subsisting in a causal and celestial manner; and in earth celestial properties, but according to a terrene condition. For how shall we account for those plants called heliotropes, that is attendants on the sun, moving in correspondence with the revolution of its orb; but selenitropes, or attendants on the moon, turning in exact conformity with her motion? it is because all things pray, and compose hymns to the leaders of their respective orders; but some intellectually, and others rationally; some in a natural, and others after a sensible manner. Hence the sunflower, as far as it is able, moves in a circular dance towards the sun; so that if any one could hear the pulsation made by its circuit in the air, he would perceive something composed by a sound of this kind, in honour of its king such as a plant is capable of framing. Hence we may behold the sun and moon in the earth, but according to a terrene quality. But in the celestial regions, all plants, and stones, and animals, possessing an intellectual life according to a celestial nature. Now the ancients having contemplated this mutual sympathy of things, applied for occult purposes both celestial and terrene natures, by means of which through a certain similitude they deduced divine virtues into this inferior abode. For indeed similitude itself is a sufficient cause of binding things together in union and consent. Thus if a piece of paper is heated, and afterwards placed near a lamp, though it does not touch the fire, the paper will be suddenly inflamed, and the flame will descend from the superior to the inferior parts. This heated paper we may compare to a certain relation of inferiors to superiors; and its approximation to the lamp, to the opportune use of things according to time, place, and matter. But the procession of fire in the paper aptly represents the presence of divine light, to that nature which is capable of its reception. Lastly, the inflammation of the paper may be compared to the deification of mortals, and to the illumination of material natures, which are afterwards carried upwards like the fire of the paper, from a certain participation of divine feed. Again, the lotus before the rising of the sun, folds its leaves into itself, but gradually expands them on its rising: unfolding them in proportion to the sun's ascent to the zenith; but as gradually contracting them as that luminary descends to the west. Hence this plant by the expansion and contraction of its leaves appears no less to honour the sun than men by the gesture of their eye-lids, and the motion of their lips. But this imitation and certain participation of supernal light is not only, visible in plants, which possess but a vestige of life, but likewise in particular stones. Thus the sun-stone, by its golden rays, imitates those of the sun; but the stone called the eye of heaven, or of the sun, has a figure similar to the pupil of an eye, and a ray shines from the middle of the pupil. Thus too the lunar stone, which has a figure similar to the moon when horned, by a certain change of itself, follows the lunar motion. Lastly, the stone called Helioselenus, i. e. of the sun and moon, imitates after a manner the congress of those luminaries, which it images by its colour. So that all things are full of divine natures; terrestrial natures receiving the plenitude of such as are celestial, but celestial of supercelestial essences; while every order of things proceeds gradually in a beautiful descent, from the highest to the lowest. For whatever is collected into one above the order of things, is afterwards dilated in descending, various souls being distributed under their various ruling divinities. In fine, some things turn round correspondent to the revolutions of the sun, and others after a manner imitate the solar rays, as the palm and the date: some the fiery nature of the sun as the laurel, and other a different property. For indeed we may perceive the properties which are collected in the sun, every where distributed to subsequent natures constituted in a solar order; that is, to angels, dæmons, souls, animals, plants, and stones. Hence the authors of the ancient priesthood, discovered from things apparent, the worship of superior powers, while they mingled some things, and purified with others. They mingled many things indeed together, because they saw that some simple substances possessed a divine property (though not taken singly) sufficient to call down that particular power, of which they were participants.

Hence by the mingling of many things together, they attracted upon us a supernal influx; and by the composition of one thing from many, they symbolised with that one, which is above many; and composed statues from the mixtures of various substances, conspiring in sympathy and consent. Besides this, they collected composite odours, by a divine art, into one, comprehending a multitude of powers, and symbolizing, with the unity of a divine essence. Considering besides, that division debilitates each of these, but that mingling them together restores them to the idea of their exemplar; hence the ancient priests, by the mutual relation and sympathy of things to one another, collected their virtues into one, but expelled them by repugnancy and antipathy; purifying, when it was requisite, with sulphur and bitumen, and the sprinkling of marine water. For sulphur purifies from the sharpness of its odour; but marine water on account of its fiery portion. Besides this, in the worship of the Gods, they offered animals, and other substances congruous to their nature; and received in the first place the powers of dæmons as proximate to natural substances and operations, by whose assistance they evocated these natural bodies to which the they approached into their presence. Afterwards they proceeded from dæmons to the powers and energies of the Gods, partly indeed from dæmoniacal instruction, but partly by their own industry, aptly interpreting symbols, and ascending to a proper intelligence of the Gods. And lastly laying aside natural substances and their operations, they received themselves into the communion and fellowship of the Gods. Thus far Proclus, and thus much for the theological doctrine of Orpheus, as contained in the works of the latter Platonists. I persuade myself enough has been said in this Dissertation to convince every thinking and liberal mind, that the Greek theology as professed and understood by the Greek philosophers, is not that absurd and nonsensical system, represented by modern prejudice and ignorance, as the creed of the ancients. In consequence of a blind and mistaken zeal it is common to ridicule the opinions of the ancient philosophers, in order to establish the certainty of the Christian religion. But surely revelation does not require so unwarrantable and feeble a support, which in reality only betrays the cause it endeavours to defend, by giving infidels occasion to suspect, either weakness in its evidence, or obscurity in its fundamental doctrines. Besides, the generality of these uncandid opponents know nothing of the Platonical writers, from whom alone genuine information can be derived on this sublime and intricate subject; and from whose works the preceding Dissertation has been so abundantly enriched. Were these invaluable books more generally known and understood, if they did not refine our taste, at present so depraved, they would at least teach us to admire the strength which human reason is capable of exerting, and to be more modest in our pretensions to wisdom; they would silence ignorant declaimers, and stop the immense increase of books on modern philosophy, which are so rapidly hastening to the abyss of forgetfulness, like streams into the ocean from which they originally flowed.

Footnotes

e In the latter part of this Dissertation, we shall discourse on the agreement between the doctrine of Orpheus and the Platonists.

f Procl. lib. i. Theol. Plat.

e Θεοι Νοεροὶ, Ὑπερκόσμιοι, Ἐγκόσμιοι Et inter hos, aliæ τάξεις Φρυρητιχῶι θεῶν, Δημιυργικῶν, Ἀναγωγῶν, Συνεκλιχῶν Τελεσιυρῶν· Ζωογόνων, Ἀλρεπλων, Ἀπολϋίων, Κριτικῶν, Καθαρλικῶν, &c. Eschenb. Epig, p. 58.

f In Timæum. p. 67.

g In Tim. p. 290.

h In Tim. p, 95.

i I have here followed the correction of Eschenbach, who reads σείρα instead of συρρα which is I think more expressive and philosophical.

k His mind is truth, and a little after, His; body full of light; or, Νοῦσ δέ ἀψευδὴς and Σωμα δέ εριψεγγὲς, perfectly agree with what Pythagoras affirmed, concerning God; that in his soul he resembled truth, and in his body light.

l Enn. 5, lib, vi.

m Vide Ἀφορμαὶ ρὸς τα Νοητά. p. 233.

n Meaning material forms and qualities.

o It is remarkable that in the Hymn to Nature, among the following, the Deity is celebrated as all things, yet the poet adds that he is alone incommunicable; which perfectly agrees with the preceding account of his subsisting in all things, and at the same time being separate and apart from all.

47

p   If the word Gods offends the ear of the reader, he may substitute in its stead, thrones, dominions; &c. for I do not discourse concerning words.
q   Stob. Ecl. Phys. p. 5.
r   En. 2. lib. ix. cap. 9.
s   In Tim. p. 286.
t   De Abstinentia, lib. i.
c   In the latter part of this Dissertation, we shall shew the wonderful agreement of the following Hymns, with the names given by Pythagoras to numbers.
x   As a Latin version only of this valuable work is published, the reader will please to make allowances for the Paraphrase, where it may be requisite.

SECT. III.

BUT it is now time to speak of the following Hymns, of which, as we have before observed, Onomacritus is the reputed author. And first, with regard to the dialect of these Hymns, Gesner well observes it ought to be no objection to their antiquity. For though, according to [x] Iamblichus, the Thracian Orpheus, who is more ancient than those noble poets Homer and Hesiod, used the Doric dialect; yet the Athenian Onomacritus, who, agreeable to the general opinion of antiquity, is the author of all the works now extant, ascribed to Orpheus [y], might either, preserving the sentences and a great part of the words, only change the dialect, and teach the ancient Orpheus to speak Homerically, or as I may say Solonically: or might arbitrarily add or take away what he thought proper, which Herodotus relates was his practice, with respect to the oracles. Gesner adds, that it does not appear probable to him that Onomacritus would dare to invent all he writ, since Orpheus must necessarily, at that time, have been in great repute, and a variety of his verses in circulation: and he concludes with observing that the objection of the Doric dialect ought to be of no more weight against the antiquity of the present works, than the Pelasgic letters, which Orpheus used according to Diodorus Siculus.

The hymns of Orpheus are not only mentioned by Plato in his Eighth Book of Laws, but also by Pausanias [a], whose words are translated as follows by the author of the Letters on Mythology [b]. "The Thracian Orpheus (says Pausanias) was represented on mount Helicon, with ΤΕΛΕΤΗ (initiation or religion) by his side, and the wild beasts of the woods, some in marble, some in bronze, standing round him. His hymns are known by those who have studied the poets to be both short and few in number. The Lycomedes, an Athenian family dedicated to sacred music, have them all by heart, and sing them at their solemn mysteries. They are but of the second class for elegance., being far excelled by Homer's in that respect. But our religion has adopted the hymns of Orpheus, and has not done the same honour to the hymns of Homer." To the testimony of Pausanias may be added that of Suidas, who, among the writings of the Libethrian Orpheus mentions τελεται, or initiations, which he says are by some ascribed to Onomacritus [c]. And Scaliger well observes, in his notes co these hymns, that they ought rather to be called initiations, because they contain only invocations of the Gods, such as the initiated in mysteries are accustomed to use; but they do not celebrate the nativities, actions, &c. of the divinities, as it is usual in hymns. It is on this account we have entitled them mystical initiations, which is doubtless their proper appellations. The author too of the Allegories in the Theogony of Hesiod [d], relating the powers of the planets on things inferior, expressly mentions these hymns, or rather initiations, and many of the compound epithets with which they abound [e]. From all which it is evident that the following Hymns were written by the Athenian Onomacritus, and are the same with those so much celebrated by antiquity. Indeed it is not probable they Should be the invention of any writer more modern than the above period, as it must have been so easy to detect the forgery, from the original initiations which were even extant at the time in which Suidas lived.

In the former part of this Dissertation, we asserted that we should derive all our information concerning the Orphic theology, from the writings of the Platonists; not indeed without reason. For this sublime theology descended from Orpheus to Pythagoras, and from Pythagoras to Plato; as the following testimonies evince. "Timæus (says Proclus) [f] being a Pythagorean, follows the Pythagoric principles, and these are the Orphic traditions; for what Orpheus delivered mystically in secret discourses, these Pythagoras learned when he was initiated by Aglaophemus in the Orphic mysteries." Syrianus too makes the Orphic and Pythagoric principles to be one and the same; and, according to Suidas, the same Syrianus composed a book, entitled the Harmony of Orpheus, Pythagoras and Plato [g]. And again Proclus [h]: it is Pythagorical to follow the Orphic genealogies; for from the Orphic tradition downward by Pythagoras, the science concerning the Gods was derived to the Greeks." And elsewhere [i], "All the theology of the Greeks is the progeny of the sacred initiations (μυσαγωγιαι) of Orpheus. For Pythagoras first learned the orgies of the Gods from Aglaophemus; but Plato was the second who received a perfect science of these, both from the Pythagoric, and Orphic writings." Now in consequence of these testimonies, our hymns ought to agree with the doctrine of Pythagoras; especially since Onomacritus, their Author, was of that school. And that .they do so, the following discovery abundantly evinces.

Photius, in his Bibliotheca, has preserved to us part of a valuable work, written by Nicomachus the Pythagorean, entitled Theological Arithmetic; in which he ascribes particular epithets, and the names of various divinities to numbers, as far as to ten. There is likewise a curious work of the same title, by an anonymous writer, which is extant only in manuscript. From these two, and from occasional passages respecting numbers according to Pythagoras, found in the Platonic writers, Meursius has composed a book, which he calls Denarius Pythagoricus; and which is an invaluable treatise to such as are studious of the ancient philosophy. On perusing this learned book, it seemed to me necessary, that as the divinities, ascribed to each number, had a particular relation to one another, they should also have a mutual agreement in the following hymns. And on the comparison I found the most perfect similitude: a few instances of which I shall select, leaving a more accurate investigation of this matter to the learned and philosophical reader.

In the first place then, among the various names ascribed to the monad or unity, are those of the following Gods; viz. the Sun, Jupiter, Love, Proteus, Vesta. Now in the hymn to the Sun we find the epithet, O immortal Jove. In that to Love πυρίδρομος, or wandering fire, which is likewise found in the hymn, to the Sun. In the hymn to Love, that deity is celebrated as having the keys of all things [k]; viz. of æther, heaven, the deep, the earth, &c. And Proteus is invoked as possessing the keys of the deep [l]. Again, Vesta, in the Orphic hymns, is the same with the mother of the Gods; and the mother of the Gods is celebrated as "always governing rivers and every sea [m]; which perfectly agrees with the appellations given both to Love and Proteus. Again, among the various epithets ascribed to the duad, or number two, are, Phanes, Nature, Justice, Rhea, Diana, Cupid, Venus, Fate, Death, &c. Now Phanes, in the Orphic hymns, is the same with Protogonus; and Nature is called πρωτογενία, or first-born, and δίκη, or Justice, as also πεπρωμενή, or Fate. Likewise Rhea is denominated θύγατερ πολυμορφυ Πωτογονοίο, or daughter, of much formed Protogonus; and in the same hymn the reader will find other epithets, which agree with the appellation given to Nature. Again, both Nature and Diana are called ὠκυλοχεία, or swiftly bringing forth; and Love as well as Nature is called or two-fold. In like manner Rhea and Venus agree, for he says of Venus πάντα γὰρ ἐκ σιθεν ἐσὶν, for all things are from thee; and of Rhea, Μήτηρ μέν τε θεῶν ἠδὲ θνητῶν ἀνθρώπων, or mother of Gods and mortal men. After which he expressly says that earth and heaven, the sea and the air, proceed from her divinity. Besides this, he celebrates Venus as governing the three Fates; αμπ ηρατέεισ τρισσῶν μοιρῶν. And lastly he says of Love, after representing that Deity as invested with the keys of all things thou alone rulest the governments of all these [n]; which he likewise affirms of Death in the same words. And thus much for the duad. The triad, or number three, they denominated Juno, Latona, Thetis, Hecate or Diana, Pluto, Tritogenia or Minerva, &c. Now Latona and Thetis, are each of them called in these initiations, κυανόπεπλ# (Οτομάκριῖθ·) or dark-veiled; and Minerva and the Moon, who is the same with Diana, θῆλωσ αμπ ἄρσην, female and male. The tetrad or number four, they denominated Hercules, Vulcan, Mercury, Bacchus two-mothered, Bassarius, key-keeper of nature, Masculine, Feminine, the World, (which in these initiations is the same with Pan) Harmony, justice. Now Onomacritus calls Hercules and Vulcan, Καρτεροχειρ, or strong-handed; and he celebrates Hercules and Mercury as "having an almighty heart." ατκρατες ἦτορ ἔχῶν. And so of the rest. The pentad or number of five they called Nature, Pallas, Immortal, Providence, Nemesis, Venus, Justice, &c. Now Nature is called in these hymns, or rather initiations πολυμήχανε μῆτερ, or much-mechanic Mother, and παντοτεχνεσ or universal Artist; and Minerva is denominated μητερ τεχνῶν, or Mother of Arts. Likewise Nature is expressly called ἀθανάτη τε ρόνιοια or Immortal, and Providence. The hexad or number six, they denominated, Venus, Health, the World Ἑκατηβελέτις darting, (because compounded of the triad, which is called Hecate), Persæa, triform, Amphitrite, &c. Now Venus, as we have already observed in the names of the duad, is said to be the source of all things and Health is expressly called μῆτερ ἀπαντων, or Mother of all things. Again the heptad, or number seven they called Fortune, Minerva, Mars., &c. And Fortune, in these initiations, is the same with Diana or the Moon, who is called male and female as well as Minerva; and Minerva and Mars are each of them denominated ὁπλιχαρές or armipotent, and Minerva πολεμοκλόνε, or full of warlike tumult. The ogdoad, or number eight, they called Rhea, Love, Neptune, Law. And the Mother of the Gods, who is the same with Rhea, is represented as we have observed on the monad, as governing rivers and every sea; and Love is said to have the keys of all things; of heaven, the deep, &c. The ennead, or number nine, they denominate Ocean, Prometheus, Vulcan, Pœan (i. e. Apollo or the Sun), Juno, Proserpine, &c. Now Saturn (who is called in these initiations Prometheus) and Ocean, are each of them celebrated as the source of Gods and men: and Vulcan is expressly called ἥλιοσ or the Sun. And lastly they denominated the decad, Heaven, the Sun, Unwearied, Fate, Phanes, Necessity, &c. Hence Heaven is called in these initiations φύλαξ πάντων, or Guardian of all things; and the Sun ισοφύλαξ, or faithful Guardian; and ἀκάμα or Unwearied, is an appellation of the Sun, in the hymn to that Deity. The reader too will find many epithets in the hymn to Protogonus or Phanes, corresponding with those of the Sun. And thus much for the agreement of these hymns, with the Pythagoric names of numbers. The limits of the present work will not permit me to be more explicit on this particular; but he who wishes to understand the meaning of many of the preceding appellations, may consult the valuable book of Meursius, already cited, where he will meet with abundant matter for deep speculation. But before I conclude this Dissertation, I must beg leave to acquaint the reader with another discovery which I have made respecting these hymns, equally curious with the former.

Ficinus, on Plato's Theology [a], has the following remarkable passage, translated, most likely from some manuscript work of Proclus, as I conjecture from its conclusion; for, unfortunately, he does not acquaint us with the author. "Those who profess, says he, the Orphic theology, consider a two-fold power in souls and in the celestial orbs: the one consisting in knowledge, the other in vivifying and governing the orb with which that power is connected. Thus in the orb of the earth, they call the nostic power Pluto, the other Proserpine [b]. In water, the former power Ocean, and the latter Thetis. In air, that thundering Jove, and this Juno. In fire, that Phanes, and this Aurora. In the soul of the lunar sphere, they call the nostic power Licnitan Bacchus, the other Thalia. In the sphere of Mercury, that Bacchus Silenus, this Euterpe. In the orb of Venus, that Lysius Bacchus, this Erato. In the sphere of the sun, that Trietericus Bacchus, this Melpomene. In the orb of Mars, that Bassareus Bacchus, this Clio. In the sphere of Jove, that Sebazius, this Terpsichore. In the orb of Saturn, that Amphietus, this Polymnia. In the eighth sphere, that Pericionius, this Urania. But in the soul of the world, the nostic power, Bacchus Eribromus, but the animating power Calliope. From all which the Orphic theologers infer, that the particular epithets of Bacchus are compared with those of the Muses on this account, that we may understand the powers of the Muses, as intoxicated with the nectar of divine knowledge; and may consider the nine Muses, and nine Bacchuses, as revolving round one Apollo, that is about the splendor of one invisible Sun." The greater part of this fine passage is preserved by Gyraldus, in his Syntagma de Musis, and by Natales Comes, in his Mythology, but without mentioning the original author. Now if the Hymn to the Earth, is compared with the Hymns to Pluto and Proserpine; the one to Ocean, with that to Thetis; and so of the other elements agreeable to the preceding account, we shall discover a wonderful similitude. And with respect to the celestial spheres, Silenus Bacchus, who, according to the preceding account, should agree with Mercury, is called in these initiations τροφὴ, or Nourishment, and Mercury, τροφιυχε, or Nourisher. Venus, who should agree with Lysius Bacchus, is called κρυφία or Occult, and ἐρατοπλόκαμος, or lovely haired, and σεμνὴ Βάκχοιο παρεδρε, or venerable attendant of Bacchus; and Lysius is denominated κρυψίγονος, or an occult offspring and καλλιέθειρα, or fair-haired. In like manner Trietericus Bacchus is called αιάν κρυσετχησ or Apollo pouring golden light, which evidently agrees with the sun. Again, Bassarius Bacchus is celebrated as rejoicing in swords and blood, οσ ξιφεσιν χαιρεισ, ἠδ' αἵμασι, κ· λ·, which plainly corresponds with Mars, as the hymn to that Deity evinces in a particular manner. Sebazius and Jupiter evidently agree, for Sebazius is expressly called ὑι# ($υἱ\ \mathfrak{D}$) Κρονυ, son of Saturn. And Amphietus is celebrated as moving in concert with the circling hours, Ἐυάζων κινῶν τε χορῦσ ἐνὶ κυκλάσιν ὥραις which corresponds with Saturn, who is called in these Hymns, or the Sun [c]. And lastly, Dionysius who is called called in these Initiations Eribromus, is denominated δικέρωτα or two-horned, which is also an epithet of Pan, or the soul of the world. And thus much for the doctrine of these Hymns, so far as is requisite to an introductory Dissertation. What farther light we have been able to. throw on these mysterious remains of antiquity, will appear in our following Notes. If the valuable Commentary of Proclus on the Cratylus of Plato was once published, I am persuaded we should find them full of the most recondite antiquity [d]: but as this is not to be expected in the present age, the lovers of ancient wisdom, will I doubt not, gratefully accept the preceding and subsequent elucidations. For on a subject so full of obscurity as the present, a glimmering light is as conspicuous, and as agreeable to the eye of the mind, as a small spark in profound darkness is to the corporeal sight.

Footnotes

x   De Vita Pythag. c. 34. p. 169. Kuft.
y   Philoponus observes, in his Commentary on Aristotle's books of the Soul, that Aristotle calls the Orphic verses reputed, because they appear not to have been written by Orpheus himself, as Aristotle affirms in his book concerning philosophy. For the Dogmata contained in them were indeed his, but Onomacritus is reported to have put them into verse.
a   In Boeoticis p. 770
b   Page 167.
c   It is remarkable that Sextus Empiricus more than once mentions Onomacritus in the Orphics. Οιομάκριλ# (*Ονομάκριλ☉*) ἐν τοῖσ Ορφικοῖσ.
d   Page 267.
e   Vide Fabric. Bib. p. 124.
f   In Timæum p. 291.
g   Συμφωνία Ορφέωσ, Πυθαγορυ, καὶ πλατονοσ.
h   In Tim. p. 289.
i   In Theol. Plat. p 13.
k   πάντων κληῖδα ἔχοντας,
    Αιθέρ# (*Αἰθέρ☉*),εραισ, κ.λ.
l   πόντυ κληῖδασ ἔχοντα.
m   Σοὶ ποτκμοὶ κροσοται ἀεὶ κ πᾶσα θάλασσα.
n   In the hymn to Love Μῦν# (*Μῦν☉*) γὰρ τύτων πάνων οἴηκα κρατύνεις. And in that to Death οἴ πάντων θητῶν οἴηκα κρατύνωεις.
a   Lib. iv. p, 128.
b   The reader may observe that this two-fold power is divided into male and female; the reason of which distribution we have already assigned from Proclus.

c   I have omitted a comparison between the eighth sphere and Pericionius from necessity, because there is no hymn among the following to that orb. And I have not contrasted Licnitan Bacchus with the lunar Sphere, because the resemblance is not apparent; though doubtless there is a concealed similitude.

d   This is evident from the following epistle of Lucas Holstenius to P. Lambecius, preserved by Fabricius in that excellent work, his Bibliotheca Græca, tom, i. p. 117 . Habeo et Orphei exemplar non contemnendum, ex quo Argonautica plurimis locis emendavi. Auctor ille huc usque a Criticorum et Correctorum vulgo derelictus tuam exposcere videtur operam. Hymni autem reconditæ antiquitatis plenissimi justum commentarium me entur, quem vel unius, Procli scripta ἀνέκδοτα tibi instruent, ut ex notis meis as Sallustium Philosophum prospicies: ne quid de cæteris, quos apud me habeo, Platonicis nunc dicam, in quibus τῆσ μυθικης θεολογίας thesaurus latet.

THE INITIATIONS OF ORPHEUS.

TO MUSÆUS *

ATTEND Musæus to my sacred song,
And learn what rites to sacrifice belong.
Jove I invoke, the earth, and solar light,
The moon's pure splendor, and the stars of night;

Thee Neptune, ruler of the sea profound, 5
Dark-hair'd, whose waves begirt the solid ground;

Ceres abundant, and of lovely mien,
And Proserpine infernal Pluto's queen
The huntress Dian, and bright Phœbus rays,
Far-darting God, the theme of Delphic praise; 10
And Bacchus, honour'd by the heav'nly choir,
And raging Mars, and Vulcan god of fire;
The mighty pow'r who rose from foam to light,
And Pluto potent in the realms of night;
With Hebe young, and Hercules the strong, 15
And you to whom the cares of births belong:
Justice and Piety august I call,
And much-fam'd nymphs, and Pan the god of all.
To Juno sacred, and to Mem'ry fair,
And the chaste Muses I address my pray'r; 20

The various year, the Graces, and the Hours,
Fair-hair'd Latona, and Dione's pow'rs;
Armed Curetes, household Gods I call,
With those who spring from Jove the king of all:
Th' Idæan Gods, the angel of the skies, 25
And righteous Themis, with sagacious eyes;
With ancient night, and day-light I implore,
And Faith, and Justice dealing right adore;
Saturn and Rhea, and great Thetis too,
Hid in a veil of bright celestial blue: 30
I call great Ocean, and the beauteous train
Of nymphs, who dwell in chambers of the main;
Atlas the strong, and ever in its prime,
Vig'rous Eternity, and endless Time;
The Stygian pool, and placid Gods beside, 35
And various Genii, that o'er men preside;

Illustrious Providence, the noble train
Of dæmon forms, who fill th' ætherial plain;
Or live in air, in water, earth, or fire,
Or deep beneath the solid ground retire. 40
Bacchus and Semele the friends of all,
And white Leucothea of the sea I call;
Palæmon bounteous, and Adrastria great,
And sweet-tongu'd Victory, with success elate;
Great Esculapius, skill'd to cure disease, 45
And dread Minerva, whom fierce battles please;
Thunders and winds in mighty columns pent,
With dreadful roaring struggling hard for vent;
Attis, the mother of the pow'rs on high,
And fair Adonis, never doom'd to die, 50
End and beginning he is all to all,

These with propitious aid I gently call;
And to my holy sacrifice invite,
The pow'r who reigns in deepest hell and night;
I call Einodian Hecate, lovely dame, 55 55
Of earthly, wat'ry, and celestial frame,
Sepulchral, in a saffron veil array'd,
Pleas'd with dark ghosts that wander thro' the shade;

Persian, unconquerable huntress hail! 59
The world's key-bearer never doom'd to fail 60
On the rough rock to wander thee delights,
Leader and nurse be present to our rites
Propitious grant our just desires success,
Accept our homage, and the incense bless.

Footnotes

* As these Hymns, though full of the most recondite antiquity, have never yet been commented on by any one, the design of the following notes, is to elucidate, as much as possible, their concealed meaning, and evince their agreement with the Platonic philosophy. Hence they will be wholly of the philosophic kind: for they who desire critical and philological information, will meet with ample satisfaction in the notes of the learned Gesner, to his excellent edition of the Orphic Remains.

The present Introduction to Musæus, the son of Orpheus, is, as Gesner observes, a summary of the work, without being servilely confined to the exact number of divinities: and the reader will please to observe through the whole of these Hymns, that the Orphic method of instruction consists in signifying divine concerns by symbols alone. And here it will be necessary to speak of philosophical mythology; as an accurate conception of its nature, will throw a general light on the Hymns, and, I hope, contribute to the dispersion of that gloom in which this sublime subject has been hitherto involved, through the barbarous systems of modern mythologists. Proclus then, on Plato's Republic, p. 170, observes, that there are two kinds of fables:

one, accommodated to puerile institution, but the other full of divine fury, which regards universal nature more than the ingenuity of the auditors. He then observes that the hearers of fables, are likewise to be distinguished: for some are of a puerile and simple ingenuity; but others are capable of rising higher, and of estimating intellectually the genera of the Gods, their progressions through all nature, and their various orders, which are extended to the utmost bounds of the universe. Hence, says he, having distributed both fable, and the hearers of fables into two parts, we cannot allow that the fables of Homer and Hesiod are accommodated to puerile institution; since they follow the nature and order of the universe, and unite with true beings such minds as are capable of being elevated to divine considerations.

Indeed nature herself, fabricating the images of intelligible essences, and of ideas totally destitute of matter, pursues this design by many and various ways. For by parts she imitates things destitute of all parts, eternal natures by such as are temporal, intelligibles by sensibles, simple essences by such as are mixt, things void of quantity by dimensions, and things stable by unceasing mutations: all which she endeavours to express as much as she is able, and as much as the aptitude of appearances will permit. Now the authors of fables, having perceived this proceeding of nature, by inventing resemblances and images of divine concerns in their verses, imitated the exalted power of exemplars by contrary and most remote adumbrations: that is, by shadowing forth the excellency of nature of the Gods by preternatural concerns: a power more divine than all reason, by such as are irrational: a beauty superior to all that is corporeal by things apparently base, and by this means placed before our eyes the excellence of divinity, which far exceeds all that can possibly be invented or said. After this, in another place of the same excellent work, he gives us some instances of the occult significations of fables: previously observing that those names which among us denote a worse condition of being, and have a worse signification, when applied to divine concerns, denote in the figments of the poets, a more excellent nature and power. Thus a bond among men, is the impediment and retention of action: but in divine concerns it insinuates a conjunction and ineffable union with causes; and hence the Saturnian bonds signify the union of the deiurgus of the universe, with the intelligible and paternal excellence of Saturn. A falling and precipitation signifies with us a violent motion; but in divine concerns, it indicates a prolific progression, and a presence every where loosened and free, which does not desert its proper principle, but depending from it pervades through every order. After this manner, the precipitation of Vulcan intimates the progression of divinity from the highest principle, to the extreme artificers of sensible things; which process is moved, perfected, and deduced from the first demiurgus and parent. Thus too castration in bodies which are composed of parts and matter, brings on a diminution of power: but in primary causes it shadows forth the progression of such as are secondary into a subject order: since primary causes revolve and produce the powers placed in their essences, yet are neither moved through the egression of secondaries, nor diminished by their separation, nor divided by the laceration of inferiors.

55 Ver. 55.] Jo Diac. Allegor. and Hesiodi Theog. p. 268. cites this line, upon which, and hymn lxxi. 3. he observes, Εὑρίσκω, τὸν Ὀξφέα καὶ τὴν ΤΥΧΗΝ ἈΡΤΕΜΙΝ προταγορεύοτα, αλλὰ καὶτη ΣΕΛΗΝΗΝ ΕΚΑΤΗΝ, i.e. "I find that Orpheus calls Fortune Artremis, or Diana, and also the Moon, Hecate."

59 Ver. 59.] Diodorus informs us that Diana, who is to be understood by this epithet, was very much worshipped by the Persians, and that this goddess was called Persæa in his Time. See more concerning this epithet in Gyrald. Syntag. ii. p. 361.

I.

TO THE GODDESS PROTHYRÆA *.

The FUMIGATION from STORAX.

O venerable goddess, hear my pray'r,
For labour pains are thy peculiar care;
in thee, when stretch'd upon the bed of grief,
The sex as in a mirror view relief.
Guard of the race, endued with gentle mind, 5
To helpless youth, benevolent and kind;
Benignant nourisher; great Nature's key
Belongs to no divinity but thee.

Thou dwell'st with all immanifest to sight,
And solemn festivals are thy delight. 10
Thine is the talk to loose the virgin's zone,
And thou in ev'ry work art seen and known.
With births you sympathize, tho' pleas'd to see
The numerous offspring of fertility;
When rack'd with nature's pangs and sore distress'd, 15
The sex invoke thee, as the soul's sure rest;
For thou alone can'st give relief to pain,
Which art attempts to ease, but tries in vain;

Assisting goddess, venerable pow'r,
Who bring'st relief in labour's dreadful hour; 20
Hear, blessed Dian, and accept my pray'r,
And make the infant race thy constant care.

Footnotes

* An epithet of Diana's, alluding to her presiding over gates, and being as it were the gate-keeper of life. It is remarkable that the first of these Hymns should be addressed to the goddess who ushers in our existence, and the last to Death. This certainly proves the collection is complete.

II.

TO NIGHT.

The FUMIGATION with TORCHES.

NIGHT, parent goddess, source of sweet repose,
From whom at first both Gods and men arose,
Hear, blessed Venus, deck'd with starry light, 3
In sleep's deep silence dwelling Ebon night!
Dreams and soft case attend thy dusky train, 5
Pleas'd with the length'ned gloom and feaftful strain.

Dissolving anxious care, the friend of Mirth,
With darkling coursers riding round the earth.
Goddess of phantoms and of shadowy play,
Whose drowsy pow'r divides the nat'ral day: 10
By Fate's decree you constant send the light
To deepest hell, remote from mortal sight
For dire Necessity which nought withstands,
Invests the world with adamantine bands.
Be present, Goddess, to thy suppliant's pray'r, 15
Desir'd by all, whom all alike revere,
Blessed, benevolent, with friendly aid
Dispell the fears of Twilight's dreadful shade.

Footnotes

3   II. Ver. 3.] See the reason why Night is called Venus, in the notes to hymn, v. to Protogonus.

III.

TO HEAVEN.

The FUMIGATION from FRANKINCENSE.

GREAT Heav'n, whose mighty frame no respite knows,
Father of all, from whom the world arose:
Hear, bounteous parent, source and end of all,
Forever whirling round this earthly ball;
Abode of Gods, whose guardian pow'r surrounds 5 5
Th' eternal World with ever during bounds;

Whose ample bosom and encircling folds
The dire necessity of nature holds.
Ætherial, earthly, whose all-various frame 9
Azure and full of forms, no power can tame. 10
All-seeing Heav'n, progenitor of Time *,
Forever blessed, deity sublime,
Propitious on a novel mystic shine,
And crown his wishes with a life divine.

Footnotes

5   III Ver. 5] Whose guardian power surrounds, &c. and v. ii. All-seeing Heaven.
ὅ τυ Ὀρφέος ὑρανὸς ὕρος καὶ πάντων φυλὰξ εἶναι βέλεται· Damascius περὶ

αρχῶν, i.e. "according to Orpheus, Heaven is the inspector and guardian of all things."

9   III. Ver. 9.] We have already observed in our Dissertation, that according to the Platonists, subordinate natures are contained in the supreme, and such as are supreme in the subordinate: and this doctrine which is originally Egyptian, is mentioned by Proclus in Tim. p. 292. as Orphical. ἔσι γὰρ καὶ ἐν γῇ ὐρανὸς καὶ ἐν ὐρανῷ γῆ, καὶ ἐνταῦθα μὲν ὁ ὐρανὸς χθονίως, εκεῖ δ'ε ὐρανίως ἡ γῆ i. e. "heaven is in earth, and earth in heaven; but here heaven subsists in an earthly manner, and there earth in a celestial manner."

*   Saturn.

IV.

TO FIRE.

The FUMIGATION from SAFFRON.

O Ever untam'd Fire, who reign'st on high
In Jove's dominions ruler of the sky;
The glorious sun with dazzling lustre bright,
And moon and stars from thee derive their light;
All taming pow'r, ætherial shining fire, 5
Whose vivid blasts the heat of life inspire:

The world's best element, light-bearing pow'r,
With starry radiance shining, splendid flow'r,
O hear my suppliant pray'r, and may thy frame
Be ever innocent, serene, and tame. 10

V.

TO PROTOGONUS,
Or the FIRST-BORN.

The FUMIGATION from MYRRH.

O Mighty first-begotten, hear my pray'r, [1]
Two-fold, egg-born, and wand'ring thro' the air,

Bull-roarer, glorying in thy golden wings, [3]
From whom the race of Gods and mortals springs.

Ericapæus, celebrated pow'r, [5]
Ineffable, occult, all shining flow'r.
From eyes obscure thou wip'st the gloom of night,
All-spreading splendour, pure and holy light
Hence Phanes call'd, the glory of the sky,
On waving pinions thro' the world you fly. [10]
Priapus, dark-ey'd splendour, thee I sing,
Genial, all-prudent, ever-blessed king,

With joyful aspect on our rights divine
And holy sacrifice propitious shine.

Footnotes

1   Ver. 1.] *First-begotten*, and v. ii. *Egg-born*. According to Orpheus, as related by Syrianus in Metaph. Aristot. p. 114, the first principle; of all things is Unity or the Good itself, and after this the Duad, or Æther and Chaos, subsists, according to Phythagoras. The first of these, or Æther, approaches to a similitude of the one itself, and is the representative of bound; the other, Chaos, comprehends in its essence multitude and infinity. Afterwards (says Syrianus) the first and secret genera of the Gods subsists, among which the first apparent is the king and father of the universe, whom on this account they call Phanes. Now this first and secret genera of the Gods, is no other than all the demiurgical and intellectual ideas, considered as proceeding to the production of the sensible World, from their occult subsistence in Æther and Chaos, whose mutual connection Orpheus represents under the symbol of an egg: upon the exclusion of which egg, by night considered as a principle, the God Phanes came forth, who is hence denominated Protogonus. Διὸ καὶ παρ Ορφεῖ ἢ Φάνης περικαλλέος αἰθέρος ηίος ονομά#εται (*ονομάζεται*), καὶ ἁβρὸς Ἔρως, Says Proclus in Tim. ii. p. 132, i. e. "on this account Phanes is called by Orpheus, the son of beautiful Æther, and tender Love." There is likewise another valuable passage on this subject from Proclus, in Tim. p. 291. as follows. "Orpheus delivers the kings of the Gods, who preside over the universe according to a perfect number; Phanes, Night, Heaven, Saturn, Jupiter, Bacchus. For Phanes is first adorned with a scepter, is the first king, and the celebrated Ericapæus. But the second king is Night, who receives the sceptre from the father Phanes. The third is Heaven, invested with government from Night. The fourth Saturn, the oppressor as they say of his father. The fifth is Jupiter, the ruler of his father. And the sixth of these is Bacchus. But all these kings having a supernal origin from the intelligible and intellectual Gods, are received into the middle orders, and in the world, both which they adorn. For Phanes is not only among the intelligible Gods, but also among the intellectual ones; in the demiurgic order, and among the super-mundane and mundane Gods. And Night and Heaven in a similar manner: for the peculiarities of these are received through all the middle orders. But with respect to the great Saturn himself, has he not an order prior to that of Jupiter, and likewise posterior to the jovial king, distributing the Dionysiacal administration (δημιυργία) together with the other Titans? and this indeed

in a different manner in the heavens and in things above the moon. And differently in the inerratic stars and in the planets; and in a similar manner Jupiter and Bacchus." Now on comparing the present hymn, and the hymns to Night, Heaven, Saturn and Jupiter together, we shall find them celebrated as the sources of all things; and Bacchus is expressly called Protogonus.

3   Ver. 3.] *Bull-roarer.* Phanes, who, according to the preceding account, is the author of the sensible world, is represented by Orpheus (for the purpose of shadowing forth the causal, not the temporal production of the universe) as adorned with the heads of a ram, a bull, a serpent, and a lion. Now Mithras, according to the Persian theology as related by Porphory de antro Nymph, is the father and creator of all things, And he informs us that the ancient priests of Ceres, called the Moon who is the queen of generation ταῦρος or a Bull (p. 262.) and p. 265 ὡς καὶ ὁ ταῦρος δημιυργὸσ ὦν ὁ Μίθρασ, καὶ γενεσέωσ δεσπότησ. i e. "Mithras as well as the Bull is the demiurgus of the universe, and the lord of generation" The reason therefore is obvious why Phanes is called Bull-roarer. Hence too from the account of Phanes given by Proclus, it follows that what that divinity is in the intelligible, that Thetis must be in the sensible world. For Thetis according to Proclus, lib. v. in Timæum is Πρετβυτάτη Θεῶν, or the most ancient and progenitor of the Gods: and Thetis is the mother of Venus, and Protogonus the father of Night. Venus therefore in the sensible world is the same as Night in the intelligible; and the reason is evident why Night in these Hymns is called Venus. I cannot conclude this note without observing how much it is to be lamented that the Platonical writers are so little known and understood in the present age. for surely if these valuable works had been consulted, it would have appeared that Protogonus and Noah resembled each other as much as the ancient and modern philosophy; or as much as an ancient commentator on Plato, and a *modern Mythology.*

VI.

TO THE STARS.

The FUMIGATION from AROMATICS.

WITH holy voice I call the stars on high,
Pure sacred lights and genii of the sky.
Celestial stars, the progeny of Night,
In whirling circles beaming far your light,
Refulgent rays around the heav'ns ye throw, 5
Eternal fires, the source of all below.
With flames significant of Fate ye shine,
And aptly rule for men a path divine.
In seven bright zones ye run with wand'ring flames,
And heaven and earth compose your lucid frames: 10
With course unwearied, pure and fiery bright
Forever shining thro' the veil of Night.
Hail twinkling, joyful, ever wakeful fires!
Propitious shine on all my just desires;

These sacred rites regard with conscious rays, 15
And end our works devoted to your praise.

Footnotes

10 Ver. 10.] *And heaven and earth*, &c. It is an Orphic and Pythagoric opinion that the stars are inhabited; on which account they are called in this hymn, earthly. But the greatest geniuses of antiquity were of the same opinion; such as Anaxagoras, Aristarchus, Heraclitus, Plato, &c. and among the Platonists not a few, as Alcinous, Plotinus, and Plutarch. Thales too is said to have called the stars earthly, by which it is probable he was of the same opinion.

VII.

TO THE SUN.

The FUMIGATION from FRANKINCENSE and MANNA.

HEAR golden Titan, whose eternal eye
With broad survey, illumines all the sky.
Self-born, unwearied in diffusing light,
And to all eyes the mirrour of delight:
Lord of the seasons, with thy fiery car 5
And leaping coursers, beaming light from far:
With thy right hand the source of morning light, 7
And with thy left the father of the night.
Agile and vig'rous, venerable Sun,
Fiery and bright around the heav'ns you run. 10
Foe to the wicked, but the good man's guide,
O'er all his steps propitious you preside:
With various founding, golden lyre, 'tis mine
To fill the world with harmony divine.

Father of ages, guide of prosp'rous deeds, 15
The world's commander, borne by lucid steeds,
Immortal Jove, all-searching, bearing light, 17
Source of existence, pure and fiery bright

Bearer of fruit, almighty lord of years,
Agil and warm, whom ev'ry pow'r reveres. 20
Great eye of Nature and the starry skies,
Doom'd with immortal flames to set and rise
Dispensing justice, lover of the stream,
The world's great despot, and o'er all supreme.
Faithful defender, and the eye of right, 25 25
Of steeds the ruler, and of life the light:
With founding whip four fiery steeds you guide,
When in the car of day you glorious ride.
Propitious on these mystic labours shine,
And bless thy suppliants with a life divine. 30

Footnotes

7   Ver. 7.] *With thy right hand,* &c. Proclus in lib. vi. Theol. Plat. P, 380, says that those who are skilled in divine concerns, attribute two hands to the Sun; denominating one the right hand, the other the left.

17   Ver. 17.] *Immortal Jove.* According to the Orphic and Platonic philosophers, the Sun is the same in the sensible, as Apollo in the intellectual, and Good in the intelligible World. Hence Proclus in Theol. Plat. p. 289. from the occult union subsisting between Good, Apollo, and the Sun, calls the Sun βασιλεὺς τυ παντὸς, or king of the universe: and it is well known that Jupiter is the demiurgus of the world. So that the Sun in perfect conformity to this Theology is called immortal Jove.

25   Ver. 25.] *Faithful defender.* Proclus, lib. v. in Timæum, in. forms us in the words of Orpheus ὅτι ἥλιον μὲν ἐπέστησε τοῖς ὅλιος, ὁ δημιυργος, και φύλακα ἀυτὸν ἔτευξε, κέλευσε τε πασιν ἀναάσσειν. "That the demiurgus placed the Sun in the universe, and fabricated him as its guardian, commanding him to govern all things."

VIII.

TO THE MOON *.

The FUMIGATION from AROMATICS.

HEAR, Goddess queen, diffusing silver light,
Bull-horn'd and wand'ring thro' the gloom of Night. 2

With stars surrounded, and with circuit wide
Night's torch extending, thro' the heav'ns you ride:
Female and Male with borrow'd rays you shine, 5 5
And now full-orb'd, now tending to decline.
Mother of ages, fruit-producing Moon,
Whose amber orb makes Night's reflected noon:

Lover of horses, splendid, queen of Night,
All-seeing pow'r bedeck'd with starry light. 10
Lover of vigilance, the foe of strife,
In peace rejoicing, and a prudent life:
Fair lamp of Night, its ornament and friend,
Who giv'st to Nature's works their destin'd end. 14
Queen of the stars, all-wife Diana hail! 15
Deck'd with a graceful robe and shining veil;
Come, blessed Goddess, prudent, starry, bright,

Come moony-lamp with chaste and splendid light,
Shine on these sacred rites with prosp'rous rays,
And pleas'd accept thy suppliant's mystic praise.

Footnotes

2   Ver. 2.] *Bull-horned*. For the mystical reason of this appellation, see note to the third line, of the Hymn to Protogonus.

*   The Moon is called in this Hymn both σελυνη and μηνη: the former of which words signifies the Moon in the language of the Gods; and the latter is the appellation given to her by Men, as the following Orphic fragment evinces.

Μήσαλο δ' ἄλλην Γᾶιαν ἀπείριτον, ἥντε Σελήνη
'Αθάνατοι κλήζυσιν, ἐπιχθόνιοι δέ τε Μηνην·
Ἡ πολλ' ὄυρε ἔχει, πολλ' ἄρεα, πολλα μέλαθρα.

That is, "But he (Jupiter) fabricated another boundless earth, which the immortals call Selene, but Men, Mene. Which has many mountains, many cities, many houses." Now this difference of names arises, according to the Platonic philosophers, from the difference subsisting between divine and human knowledge. For (say they) as the knowledge of the Gods is different from that of particular souls: so with respect to names some are diverse, exhibiting the whole essence of that which is named; but others are human, which only partially unfolds their signification. But a larger account of this curious particular, is given by Proclus, in Theol. Plat. p. 69. as follows. There are three kinds of names: the first and most proper, and which are truly divine, subsist in the Gods themselves. But the second which are the resemblances of the first, having an intellectual subsistence, must be esteemed of divine condition. And the third kind which emanate from Truth itself, but are formed into words for the purpose of discourse, receiving the last signification of divine concerns, are enunciated by skillful men at one time by a divine afflatus, at another time by energising intellectually, and generating the images of internal spectacles moving in a discursive procession. For as the demiurgic intellect represents about matter the significations of primary forms comprehended in its essence; temporal signatures of things eternal; divisible representatives of things in divisible, and produces as it were shadowy resemblances of true beings: after the same manner I think the science we possess, framing an intellectual action, fabricates by discourse both the resemblances of other things, and of the Gods themselves. So that it fashions by composition, that which in the Gods is void of composition; that which is simple by variety; and that which is united by multitude. And by this formation of names it demonstrates in the last place the images of divine concerns. And as the theurgic art provokes by certain signs, supernal illumination into artificial statutes, and allures the unevnying goodness of the Gods, in the same manner the science of divine concerns, signifies the occult essence of the God by the compositions and divisions of sounds.

5   Ver. 5.] Female and Male. This is not wonderful, since according to the fragment of Ficinus in this Dissertation, all souls and the celestial spheres are endued with a two-fold power, nostic and animating; one of which is male and the other female. And these epithets are perpetually occurring in the Orphic Initiations.

14   Ver. 14.] *Who giv'st to Nature's works*, &c. In the original it is τελεσφορος, i. e. bringing to an end. And Proclus in Theol. Plat. p. 483. informs us that Diana (who is the same with the Moon) is so called, because she finishes or perfects the essential perfection of matter.

IX.

TO NATURE. *

The FUMIGATION from AROMATICS.

NATURE, all parent, ancient, and divine,
O Much-mechanic mother, art is thine;

Heav'nly, abundant, venerable queen,
In ev'ry part of thy dominions seen.

Untam'd, all-taming, ever splendid light, 5
All ruling, honor'd, and supremly bright.
Immortal, first-born, ever still the same,
Nocturnal, starry, shining, glorious dame.
Thy feet's still traces in a circling course,
By thee are turn'd, with unremitting force. 10
Pure ornament of all the pow'rs divine,
Finite and infinite alike you shine; 12
To all things common and in all things known,
Yet incommunicable and alone.
Without a father of thy wond'rous frame, 15
Thyself the father whence thy essence came.
All-flourishing, connecting, mingling soul,

Leader and ruler of this mighty whole.
Life-bearer, all-sustaining, various nam'd,
And for commanding grace and beauty fam'd. 20
Justice, supreme in might, whose general sway
The waters of the restless deep obey.
Ætherial, earthly, for the pious glad,
Sweet to the good, but bitter to the bad.
All-wife, all bounteous, provident, divine, 25
A rich increase of nutriment is thine;

Father of all, great nurse, and mother kind,
Abundant, blessed, all-spermatic mind:
Mature, impetuous, from whose fertile seeds
And plastic hand, this changing scene proceeds. 30
All-parent pow'r, to mortal eyes unseen,
Eternal, moving, all-sagacious queen.
By thee the world, whose parts in rapid flow, 33
Like swift descending streams, no respite know,
On an eternal hinge, with steady course 35
Is whirl'd, with matchless, unremitting force.
Thron'd on a circling car, thy mighty hand
Holds and directs, the reins of wide command.
Various thy essence, honor'd, and the best,
Of judgement too, the general end and test. 40

Intrepid, fatal, all-subduing dame,
Life-everlasting, Parca, breathing flame.
Immortal, Providence, the world is thine,
And thou art all things, architect divine.
O blessed Goddess, hear thy suppliant's pray'r, 45
And make my future life, thy constant care;

Give plenteous seasons, and sufficient wealth,
And crown my days with lasting, peace and health.

Footnotes

* Nature, according to the theologists, as related by Proclus, in Tim. p. iv. is the last of the demiurgic causes of this sensible world, and the boundary of the latitude of incorporeal essences: and is full of reasons and powers, by which she governs the universe, every where connecting parts with their wholes. Hence Nature is represented in this Hymn as turning the still traces of her feet with a swift whirling. For since she is the last of the demiurgic causes, her operations aptly symbolize with the traces of feet. Now the reason why the epithets of much-mechanic, all-artist, connecting, all-wife, providence, &c. are given to nature, which evince her agreement with Minerva, is because that Goddess, according to the Orphic theology, fabricated the variegated veil of nature, from that wisdom and virtue of which she is the presiding divinity. And Proclus in forms us, that she connects all the parts of the universe together: containing in herself intellectual life, by which she illuminates the whole, and unifying powers by which she superintends all the opposing natures of the world. Nature, therefore, from her connecting, and unifying power, and from her plenitude of seminal reasons, has an evident agreement with Minerva, whose divine arts according to the Orphic theology, reduce whatever in the universe is discordant and different, into union and consent.

Again, agreeable to this theology, primary natures impart their gifts to such as are secondary by an abundant illumination, and effects are established in the causes from which they proceed: so that in the obscure language of Heraclitus, all things are one, and one all things. Hence Nature though the last of the demiurgic causes, is with perfect conformity to this symbolical Theology, said to be both communicable and incommunicable; without a father and at the same time the father of her own being. For considered as full of operative reasons, she is communicable to every sensible nature: but considered as the representative of divine unity, she is incommunicable. And in like manner as symbolising with the first cause, she is both without any origin, and at the same time the source of her own essence.

12 Ver. 12.] Finite and infinite, &c. Philolaus according to Demetrius (in Laert.) published a discourse concerning Nature, of which this is the beginning φύσις

δὲ ἐν τῳ κόσμῳ ἁρμόχθη ἐξ ἁ ειρηον τε καὶ ὅλ# (ὅλος) κόσμοσ καὶ τὰ ἐν αυτῳ παντα. i. e. "Nature, and the whole world, and whatever it contains. are aptly connected together from infinites and finites."

33 Ver. 33.] *By thee the world*, &c. Since the world has an extended and composite essence, and is on this account continually separated from itself, it can alone be connected by a certain indivisible virtue infused from the divine unity. Again, since from a natural appetite, it is ever orderly moved towards good, the nature of such an appetite and motion must originate from a divine intellect and goodness. But since, from its material imperfection, it cannot receive the whole of divine infinity at once, but in a manner accommodated to its temporal nature: it can only derive it gradually and partially, as it were by drops, in a momentary succession. So that the corporeal world is in a continual state of flowing and formation, but never possesses real being; and is like the image of a lofty tree seen in a rapid torrent, which has the appearance of a tree without the reality; and which seems to endure perpetually the same, yet is continually renewed by the continual renovation of the stream.

X.

TO PAN *

The FUMIGATION from VARIOUS ODORS

I Call strong Pan, the substance of the whole,
Etherial, marine, earthly, general soul,
Immortal fire; for all the world is thine,
And all are parts of thee, O pow'r divine.

Come, blessed Pan, whom rural haunts delight, 5
Come, leaping, agile, wand'ring, starry light;
The Hours and Seasons, wait thy high command,
And round thy throne in graceful order stand.
Goat-footed, horned, Bacchanalian Pan,
Fanatic pow'r, from whom the world began, 10
Whose various parts by thee inspir'd, combine
In endless dance and melody divine.
In thee a refuge from our fears we find,
Those fears peculiar to the human kind.
Thee shepherds, streams of water, goats rejoice, 15
Thou. lov'st the chace, and Echo's secret voice: 16
The sportive nymphs, thy ev'ry step attend, 17
And all thy works fulfill their destin'd end.

O all-producing pow'r, much-fam'd, divine,
The world's great ruler, rich increase is thine. 20
All-fertile Pæan, heav'nly splendor pure,
In fruits rejoicing, and in caves obscure. 22
True serpent-horned Jove, whose dreadful rage 23
When rous'd, 'tis hard for mortals to asswage.
By thee the earth wide-bosom'd deep and long, 25
Stands on a basis permanent and strong.
Th' unwearied waters of the rolling sea,
Profoundly spreading, yield to thy decree.
Old Ocean too reveres thy high command,
Whose liquid arms begirt the solid land. 30
The spacious air, whose nutrimental fire,
And vivid blasts, the heat of life inspire
The lighter frame of fire, whose sparkling eye
Shines on the summit of the azure sky,
Submit alike to thee, whole general sway 35
All parts of matter, various form'd obey.

All nature's change thro' thy protecting care,
And all mankind thy lib'ral bounties share:
For these where'er dispers'd thro' boundless space,
Still find thy providence support their race. 40
Come, Bacchanalian, blessed power draw near,
Fanatic Pan, thy humble suppliant hear,
Propitious to these holy rites attend,
And grant my life may meet a prosp'rous end;
Drive panic Fury too, wherever found, 55
From human kind, to earth's remotest bound.

Footnotes

*   Pan, it is well known, is the same with the Universe, and is called by Orpheus προτογονοσ (Protogonos), as we are informed by Damascius περὶ ἀρχῶν. Now Jupiter in the Orphic theology, is the demiurgus of the universe, or the first intellect; and Apollo, in the intellectual world, is the same with Jupiter, as we have shewn in our notes to the Sun. Hence the reason is obvious why Pan is called in this Hymn, all-fertile Pan. And if we compare the Orphic fragment, given in the Dissertation, with the present Hymn, we shall find a striking resemblance; as the king and father of universe, Protogonus or Jupiter is there celebrated as being all things; and is represented under the symbol of a divine body, whole members are the various parts of the world.

16 Ver. 16] *Echo's secret voice*. Phurnutus informs us, that Pan is reported to dwell in solitary places, for the purpose of evincing his unity. For the World is one, and only-begotten. Opusc. Mythol. p. 203.

17 Ver. 17] *The sportive nymphs*. This is because Pan rejoices in the exhalations produced from humid substances; without which the world cannot subsist. *Phurnutus.*

22 Ver. 22.] *In caves obscure*. A cave, as we learn from Porphyry, de Antro Nympharum, is an apt symbol of the material world; since it is agreeable at its first entrance on account of its participation of form, but is involved in the deepest obscurity to the intellectual eye, which endeavours to discern its dark foundation. So that, like a cave, its exterior and superficial parts are pleasant; but its interior parts are obscure, and its very bottom, darkness itself.

23 Ver 23.] *True serpent-horned Jove*. The reason why Pan is horned, is, because Jove is the mingler of all things, according to Orpheus, as we learn from Jo. Diac. Allegor. in Hesiod. p. 305; and the word κερασήσ is as Gesner observes, derived from the verb κεράννυμι, to mingle: so that horns are an occult symbol of the mingling and tempering power of the demiurgus of the world. But the literal meaning of the word κερασήσ is horned serpent; and one of the heads of Protogonus is that of a serpent. We may add that Pan considered as the soul of the world, is with great propriety called Jove; since that appellation is given by Orpheus to the mundane soul.

XI.

TO HERCULES.

The FUMIGATION from FRANKINCENSE.

HEAR, pow'rful, Hercules untam'd and strong,
To whom vast hands, and mighty works belong,
Almighty Titan, prudent and benign,
Of various forms, eternal and divine,
Father of Time, the theme of gen'ral praise, 5
Ineffable, ador'd in various ways.
Magnanimous, in divination skill'd
And in the athletic labours of the field.
'Tis thine strong archer, all things to devour,
Supreme, all-helping, all-producing pow'r; 10
To thee mankind as their deliv'rer pray,
Whose arm can chase the savage tribes away:

Uweary'd, earth's best blossom, offspring fair,
To whom calm peace, and peaceful works are dear. 13
Self-born, with primogenial fires you shine, 15 15
And various names and strength of heart are thine.
Thy mighty head supports the morning light,
And bears untam'd, the silent gloomy night;

From east to west endu'd with strength divine,
Twelve glorious labours to absolve is thine; 20

Supremely skill'd, thou reign'st in heav'n's abodes,
Thyself a God amid'st th' immortal Gods.
With arms unshaken, infinite, divine,
Come, blessed pow'r, and to our rites incline;
The mitigations of disease convey, 25
And drive disasterous maladies away.
Come, shake the branch with thy almighty arm,
Dismiss thy darts and noxious fate disarm.

Footnotes

13 Ver. 13] *Earth's best blossom*. Since, according to the Orphic theology, there are two worlds, the intelligible and the sensible, the former of which is the source of the latter; so, according to the same theology, the first contains in a primary, causal, and intellectual manner, what the second comprehends secondarily and sensibly. Hence it contains an intellectual heaven and earth, not like the material, existing in place, and affected with the circulations of Time; but subsisting immaterially in the stable essence of eternity. In this divine world, another sun, and moon, and stars shine with intellectual light; for every thing there is perfectly lucid, light continually mingling with light. There, as Plotinus divinely observes, every star is a sun: and though all things are beheld in every thing, yet some things are more excellent than others. Now from this intellectual heaven and earth, resident in Phanes, the king and father of the universe, Orpheus, according to Proclus, derives the orders of the Gods, subordinate to this sensible heaven and earth: and among these he relates the following progeny of the intellectual earth, as preserved by Proclus in his excellent Commentary on the Timæus, p. 295, and by Athenagoras in Apol. "She produced seven beautiful pure virgins with voluble eyes, and seven sons, all of them kings, and covered with downy hair; the daughters are Themis and prudent Tethys, and fair-haired Mnemosyne, and blessed Thea; together with Dione, having an illustrious form, and Phœbe and Rhea the mother of

king Jupiter. But this illustrious earth generated celestial sons, which are also sirnamed Titans, because they took revenge on the great starry heaven; and these are Cæus and great Cræus, and robust Phorcys, and Saturn, and Ocean, and Hyperion, and Iapetus." Now Hercules is celebrated in this Hymn as the Sun, as the nineteenth and twentieth lines particularly evince; and the Sun is the same with Hyperion; hence the reason is obvious why Hercules is called "earth's best blossom." And we shall find that Saturn in the following hymn is called "blossom of the earth;" and Themis, in Hymn 78, "young blossom of the earth;" and the Titans, in Hymn 36, "the illustrious progeny of heaven and earth."

15 Ver. 15.] *With primogenial fires you shine.* Since the intelligible world, which, as we have already observed, was produced from Æther and Chaos, is nothing else than the comprehension of all the demiurgic ideas in the divine mind, which is, according to Orpheus, the God Phanes; it remains that the sensible world, which is but the image τυ Νοζτυ Παραδείγματοσ of an intelligible paradigm, should be produced according to its similitude, and filled with its proper divinities. Now Phanes, the author of the sensible world, is represented by Orpheus (for the purpose of symbolically representing the causal production of the universe) as adorned with the heads of various animals. According to Athenagoras, with the head of a dragon, of a lion, and the countenance of the God himself; but according to Proclus and others, in the words of Orpheus, with the countenance of a ram, a bull, a serpent and a lion. And this Phanes Athenagoras informs us is denominated by Orpheus, Hercules, and Time. Hence we see the reason why Hercules is said to shine with primogenial fires; since he is no other than Protogonos in the intelligible, and the Sun in the sensible world. Hence too the reason is apparent why Saturn who is the same with Time, is called in the following Hymn, τιτὰν i.e. Titan, or the Sun.

XII.

TO SATURN.

The FUMIGATION from STORAX.

ETHERIAL father, mighty Titan, hear, 1
Great fire of Gods and men, whom all revere:
Endu'd with various council, pure and strong,
To whom perfection and decrease belong.
Consum'd by thee all forms that hourly die, 5
By thee restor'd, their former place supply;
The world immense in everlasting chains,
Strong and ineffable thy pow'r contains
Father of vast eternity, divine,
O mighty Saturn, various speech is thine: 10
Blossom of earth and of the starry skies,
Husband of Rhea, and Prometheus wife.

Obstetric Nature, venerable root,
From which the various forms of being shoot;
No parts peculiar can thy pow'r enclose, 15
Diffus'd thro' all, from which the world arose,
O, best of beings, of a subtle mind,
Propitious hear to holy pray'rs inclin'd;

The sacred rites benevolent attend,
And grant a blameless life, a blessed end.

Footnotes

1   Ver. 1.] *Mighty Titan*. See the notes to the preceding hymn.

XIII.

TO RHEA *.

The FUMIGATION from AROMATICS.

DAUGHTER of great Protogonus, divine, 1
Illustrious Rhea, to my pray'r incline,

Who driv'st thy holy car with speed along,
Drawn by fierce lions, terrible and strong. 4
Mother of Jove, whose mighty arm can wield 5
Th' avenging bolt, and shake the dreadful shield.
Drum-beating, frantic, of a splendid mien, 7
Brass-sounding, honor'd, Saturn's blessed queen.
Thou joy'st in mountains and tumultuous fight,
And mankind's horrid howlings, thee delight. 10

War's parent, mighty, of majestic frame,
Deceitful saviour, liberating dame. 12
Mother of Gods and men, from whom the earth
And lofty heav'ns derive their glorious birth;
Th' ætherial gales, the deeply spreading sea 15
Goddess ærial form'd, proceed from thee.
Come, pleas'd with wand'rings, blessed and divine,

With peace attended on our labours shine;
Bring rich abundance, and wherever found
Drive dire disease, to earth's remotest bound. 20

Footnotes

1 Ver. 1.] *Daughter of great Protogonus.* In the note to Hercules it appears that Rhea is one of the progeny of the intellectual earth, resident in Phanes; and from the note to Hymn 5, to Protogonus, we learn from Proclus, that Phanes is to be considered in the intelligible as well as in the intellectual orders. Hence Rhea is, with perfect agreement to the Orphic theology, the daughter of Protogonus, considered as subsisting among the intelligible Gods.

* Rhea, according to the Orphic and Platonic theology, is one of the zoogonic or vivific principles of the universe; having a maternal rank among the universal paternal orders, i. e. between Saturn and Jupiter. Hence she calls forth the causes latent in Saturn to the procreation of the universe; and definitely unfolds all the genera of the Gods. So that she is filled from Saturn, with an intelligible and prolific power, which she imparts to Jupiter the demiurgus of the universe; filling his essence with a vivific abundance. Since this Goddess then is a medium between the two intellectual parents of the universe, Saturn and Jupiter, the former of which collects intellectual multitude into one, but the other scatters and divides it. Hence says Proclus, in Theol. Plat. p. 266. this Goddess produces in herself the demiurgic causes of the universe; but imparts her diffusive power abundantly to secondary natures. On this account Plato assimilates her prolific abundance to the flowing of waters; signifying nothing more by the word *flowing*, than that fontal power, by which she singularly contains the divine rivers of life. And, p. 267. Proclus informs us, that this Goddess, according to Orpheus, when considered as united to Saturn by the most exalted part of her essence, is called Rhea: but considered as producing Jupiter, and, together with Jove, unfolding the universal and particular orders of the Gods, she is called Ceres.

4 Ver. 4.] *Drawn by fierce lions*, &c. I have here followed the correction of Pierson, who reads ταυροφονων for ταυροφορον: for Rhea is the same with the mother of the Gods, who is celebrated in the Hymn to her, as seated in a car drawn by lions.

7   Ver. 7.] *Drum-beating.* Rhea, in the Orphic theology, is among the mundane divinities, the earth. Hence, according to Varro, she is represented with a drum; because that instrument is a symbol of the earth. August. de Civitat. lib. vii.

12   XIII Ver. 12.] *Deceitful saviour.* When Jupiter was born (says the fable) his mother Rhea in order to deceive Saturn, gave him a stone wrapped in swaddling bands, in the place of Jove; informing him that was her offspring. Saturn immediately devoured the stone; and Jupiter who was privately educated, at length obtained the government of the world. With great propriety, therefore, is she called by the poet a deceitful saviour. This fable, according to Phurnutus, signifies the creation of the world. For at that time Nature (which among elementary essences is the same with Jupiter) was then nourished in the world, and at length prevailed. The stone devoured by Saturn is the earth, alluding to its firmly occupying the middle place: for says Phurnutus, beings could not abide without such a foundation for their support. From this all things are produced, and derive their proper aliment. Opusc. Mythol. p. 147.

XIV.

TO JUPITER.

The FUMIGATION from STORAX.

O Jove much-honor'd, Jove supremely great,
To thee our holy rites we consecrate,

Our pray'rs and expiations, king divine,
For all things round thy head exalted shine.
The earth is thine, and mountains swelling high, 5
The sea profound, and all within the sky.
Saturnian king, descending from above,
Magnanimous, commanding, sceptred Jove;
All-parent, principle and end of all,
Whose pow'r almighty, shakes this earthly ball; 10
Ev'n Nature trembles at thy mighty nod,
Loud-sounding, arm'd with light'ning, thund'ring God.
Source of abundance, purifying king,
O various-form'd from whom all natures spring;
Propitious hear my pray'r, give blameless health, 15
With peace divine, and necessary wealth.

XV.

TO JUNO *.

The FUMIGATION from AROMATICS.

O Royal Juno of majestic mien,
Aerial-form'd, divine, Jove's blessed queen,
Thron'd in the bosom of cærulean air,
The race of mortals is thy constant care.

The cooling gales thy pow'r alone inspires,
Which nourish life, which ev'ry life desires.
Mother of clouds and winds, from thee alone
Producing all things, mortal life is known:
All natures share thy temp'rament divine,
And universal sway alone is thine. 10
With founding blasts of wind, the swelling sea
And rolling rivers roar, when shook by thee.
Come, blessed Goddess, fam'd almighty queen,
With aspect kind, rejoicing and serene.

Footnotes

* Juno is called by the Orphic theologers, according to Proclus Ζωογόνος θεά or the vivific Goddess: an epithet perfectly agreeing with the attributes ascribed to her in this Hymn. And in Theol. Plat. p. 483, he says that Juno is the source of the soul's procreation.

XVI.

TO NEPTUNE.

The FUMIGATION from MYRRH

HEAR, Neptune, ruler of the sea profound,
Whose liquid grasp begirts the solid ground;
Who, at the bottom of the stormy main,
Dark and deep-bosom'd, hold'st thy wat'ry reign;
Thy awful hand the brazen trident bears,
And ocean's utmost bound, thy will reveres:
Thee I invoke, whose steeds the foam divide,
From whose dark locks the briny waters glide;
Whose voice loud founding thro' the roaring deep,
Drives all its billows, in a raging heap; 10
When fiercely riding thro' the boiling sea,
Thy hoarse command the trembling waves obey.

Earth shaking, dark-hair'd God, the liquid plains
(The third division) Fate to thee ordains,
'Tis thine, cærulian dæmon, to survey
Well pleas'd the monsters of the ocean play, 15
Confirm earth's basis, and with prosp'rous gales

Waft ships along, and swell the spacious sails;
Add gentle Peace, and fair-hair'd Health beside,
And pour abundance in a blameless tide. 20

XVII.

TO PLUTO.

PLUTO, magnanimous, whose realms profound
Are fix'd beneath the firm and solid ground,
In the Tartarian plains remote from fight,
And wrapt forever in the depths of night;
Terrestrial Jove, thy sacred ear incline, 5
And, pleas'd, accept thy mystic's hymn divine.
Earth's keys to thee, illustrious king belong,
Its secret gates unlocking, deep and strong.
'Tis thine, abundant annual fruits to bear,
For needy mortals are thy constant care. 10

To thee, great king, Avernus is assign'd,
The seat of Gods, and basis of mankind.
Thy throne is fix'd in Hade's dismal plains,
Distant, unknown to rest, where darkness reigns;
Where, destitute of breath, pale spectres dwell, 15
In endless, dire, inexorable hell;
And in dread Acheron, whose depths obscure,
Earth's stable roots eternally secure.
O mighty dæmon, whose decision dread,
The future fate determines of the dead, 20
With captive Proserpine, thro' grassy plains,

Drawn in a four-yok'd car with loosen'd reins,
Rapt o'er the deep, impell'd by love, you flew
'Till Eleusina's city rose to view;
There, in a wond'rous cave obscure and deep, 25
The sacred maid secure from search you keep,
The cave of Atthis, whose wide gates display
An entrance to the kingdoms void of day.
Of unapparent works, thou art alone
The dispensator, visible and known. 30
O pow'r all-ruling, holy, honor'd light,
Thee sacred poets and their hymns delight:
Propitious to thy mystic's works incline,
Rejoicing come, for holy rites are thine.

Footnotes

5 Ver. 5.] *Terrestrial Jove*, Pluto, says Proclus in Theol. Plat. p. 368. is called terrestrial Jupiter, because he governs by his providence the earth, and all she contains.

7 Ver. 7.] *Earth's keys*. Pausanias informs us, that Pluto is reported to have keys, as an illustrious distinction; in the same manner as a sceptre is attributed to Jupiter, and a trident to Neptune.

XVIII.

TO THUNDRING JOVE.

The FUMIGATION from STORAX.

O Father Jove, who shak'st with fiery light
The world deep-sounding from thy lofty height:
From thee, proceeds th' ætherial lightning's blaze,
Flashing around intolerable rays.
Thy sacred thunders shake the blest abodes, 5
The shining regions of th' immortal Gods:
Thy pow'r divine, the flaming lightning shrouds,
With dark investiture, in fluid clouds.
'Tis thine to brandish thunders strong and dire,
To scatter storms, and dreadful darts of fire; 10
With roaring flames involving all around,
And bolts of thunder of tremendous sound.
Thy rapid dart can raise the hair upright,
And shake the heart of man with wild afright.
Sudden, unconquer'd, holy, thund'ring God, 15
'With noise unbounded, flying all abroad;
With all-devouring force, entire and strong,
Horrid, untam'd, thou roll'st the flames along.
Rapid, ætherial bolt, descending fire,

The earth all-parent, trembles at thy ire; 20
The sea all-shining; and each beast that hears
The sound terrific, with dread horror fears:
When Nature's face is bright with flashing fire,
And in the heavens resound thy thunders dire.

Thy thunders white, the azure garments tear,
And burst the veil of all surrounding air.
O Jove, all-blessed, may thy wrath severe,
Hurl'd in the bosom of the deep appear,
And on the tops of mountains be reveal'd,
For thy strong arm is not from us conceal'd. 30
Propitious to these sacred rites incline,
And crown my wishes with a life divine:
Add royal health, and gentle peace beside,
With equal reason, for my constant guide.

XIX.

To JOVE, as the AUTHOR of LIGHTNING.

The FUMIGATION from FRANKINCENSE and MANNA.

I Call the mighty, holy, splendid light,
Aerial, dreadful-sounding, fiery-bright;
Flaming, aerial-light, with angry voice,
Lightning thro' lucid clouds with horrid noise.
Untam'd, to whom resentments dire belong,
Pure, holy pow'r, all-parent, great and strong:
Come, and benevolent these rites attend,
And grant my days a peaceful, blessed end.

XX.

TO THE CLOUDS.

The FUMIGATION from MYRRH.

Ærial clouds, thro' heav'n's resplendent plains
Who wander, parents of prolific rains;
Who nourish fruits, whose water'y frames are hurl'd,
By winds impetuous, round the mighty world;
All-thund'ring, lion-roaring, flashing fire, 5
In Air's wide bosom, bearing thunders dire
Impell'd by ev'ry stormy, sounding gale,
With rapid course, along the skies ye fail.
With blowing winds your wat'ry frames I call,
On mother Earth with fruitful show'rs to fall.

XXI.

TO THE SEA, OR TETHYS *.

The FUMIGATION from FRANKINCENSE and MANNA.

TETHYS I call, with eyes cærulean bright,
Hid in a veil obscure from human sight;
Great Ocean's empress, wand'ring thro' the deep,
And pleas'd with gentle gales, the earth to sweep;

Whose blessed waves in swift succession go, 5
And lash the rocky shore with endless flow:
Delighting in the Sea serene to play,
In ships exulting and the wat'ry way.
Mother of Venus, and of clouds obscure,
Great nurse of beasts, and source of fountains pure. 10
O venerable Goddess, hear my pray'r,
And make benevolent my life thy care;
Send, blessed queen, to ships a prosp'rous breeze,
And waft them safely o'er the stormy seas.

Footnotes

* See the last note to Hymn v. for an explanation of the Goddess Tethys.

XXII.

TO NEREUS.

The FUMIGATION from MYRRH.

O Thou, who doff the roots of Ocean keep
In seats cærulean, dæmon of the deep,
With fifty nymphs (attending in thy train,
Fair virgin artists) glorying thro' the main:
The dark foundation of the rolling sea 5
And Earth's wide bounds, belong much-fam'd to thee;
Great dæmon, source of all, whose pow'r can make
The Earth's unmeasur'd, holy basis shake,
When blust'ring winds in secret caverns pent,
By thee excited, struggle hard for vent: 10
Come, blessed Nereus, listen to my pray'r,
And cease to shake the earth with wrath severe;

Send on our sacred rites abundant health,
With peace divine and necessary wealth.

XXIII.

TO THE NEREIDS.

The FUMIGATION from AROMATICS.

DAUGHTERS of Nereus, resident in caves
Merg'd deep in Ocean, sporting thro' the waves;
Fanatic fifty nymphs, who thro' the main
Delight to follow in the Triton's train,
Rejoicing close behind their cars to keep; 5
Whose forms half wild, are nourish'd by the deep,
With other nymphs of different degree
Leaping and wand'ring thro' the liquid sea:
Bright, wat'ry dolphins, sonorous and gay,
Well pleas'd to sport with bachanalian play; 10
Nymphs beauteous-ey'd, whom sacrifice delights,
Send rich abundance on our mystic rites;
For you at first disclos'd the rites divine,
Of holy Bacchus and of Proserpine,
Of fair Calliope from whom I spring, 15
And of Apollo bright, the Muse's king.

XXIV.

TO PROTEUS [*].

The FUMIGATION from STORAX.

PROTEUS I call, whom Fate decrees, to keep
The keys which lock the chambers of the deep;
First-born, by whose illustrious pow'r alone
All Nature's principles are clearly shewn:
Matter to change with various forms is thine, 5
Matter unform'd, capacious, and divine.
All-honor'd, prudent, whose sagacious mind
Knows all that was, and is, of ev'ry kind,
With all that shall be in succeeding time;
So vast thy wisdom, wond'rous, and sublime: 10
For all things Nature first to thee consign'd,
And in thy essence omniform confin'd.
Come, blessed father, to our rites attend,
And grant our happy lives a prosp'rous end.

Footnotes

[*] According to Proclus, in Plat. Repub. p. 97, Proteus, though inferior to the primary Gods, is immortal: and though not a deity, is a certain angelic mind of the order of Neptune, comprehending in himself all the forms of things generated in the universe.

XXV.

TO THE EARTH *

The FUMIGATION from every kind of SEED,
except BEANS and AROMATICS.

O Goddess, Earth, of Gods and men the source,
Endu'd with fertile, all destroying force;
All-parent, bounding, whose prolific pow'rs,
Produce a store of beauteous fruits and flow'rs,
All-various maid, th' eternal world's strong base 5
Immortal, blessed, crown'd with ev'ry grace;
From whose wide womb, as from an endless root,
Fruits, many-form'd, mature and grateful shoot.
Deep bosom'd, blessed, pleas'd with grassy plains,
Sweet to the smell, and with prolific rains. 10
All flow'ry dæmon, centre of the world,
Around thy orb, the beauteous stars are hurl'd
With rapid whirl, eternal and divine,
Whose frames with matchless skill and wisdom shine.
Come, blessed Goddess, listen to my pray'r, 15
And make increase of fruits thy constant care;
With fertile Seasons in thy train, draw near,
And with propitious mind thy suppliant hear.

Footnotes

*   According to Orpheus, as related by Proclus, in Tim. p. 292. Earth is the mother of every thing, of which Heaven is the father. And the reader will please to observe, that, in the Orphic theology, Rhea, the mother of the Gods, the Earth, and Vesta, are all one and the same divinity, considered according to her essential peculiarities.

XXVI.

TO THE MOTHER OF THE GODS.

The FUMIGATION from a
Variety of ODORIFEROUS SUBSTANCES.

Mother of Gods, great nurse of all, draw near,
Divinely honor'd, and regard my pray'r:
Thron'd on a car, by lions drawn along,
By bull-destroying lions, swift and strong,
Thou sway'st the sceptre of the pole divine, 5
And the world's middle seat, much-fam'd, is thine.
Hence earth is thine, and needy mortals share
Their constant food, from thy protecting care:
From thee at first both Gods and men arose;
From thee, the sea and ev'ry river flows. 10
Vesta, and source of good, thy name we find
To mortal men rejoicing to be kind;
For ev'ry good to give, thy soul delights;
Come, mighty pow'r, propitious to our rites,
All-taming, blessed, Phrygian saviour, come, 15
Saturn's great queen, rejoicing in the drum.

Celestial, ancient, life-supporting maid,
Fanatic Goddess, give thy suppliant aid;

With joyful aspect on our incense shine,
And, pleas'd, accept the sacrifice divine.

Footnotes

5 Ver. 5.] We have already observed, that the mother of the Gods is the same with Rhea; and Proclus, in the second book of his Commentary on Euclid, informs us, that the pole of the world is called by the Pythagoreans the seal of Rhea.

XXVII.

TO MERCURY.

The FUMIGATION from FRANKINCENSE.

HERMES, draw near, and to my pray'r incline,
Angel of Jove, and Maia's son divine;
Studious of contests, ruler of mankind,
With heart almighty, and a prudent mind.
Celestial messenger, of various skill, 5
Whose pow'rful arts could watchful Argus kill:
With winged feet, 'tis thine thro' air to course,
O friend of man, and prophet of discourse:
Great life-supporter, to rejoice is thine,
In arts gymnastic, and in fraud divine: 10
With pow'r endu'd all language to explain,
Of care the loos'ner, and the source of gain.
Whose hand contains of blameless peace the rod,
Corucian, blessed, profitable God;
Of various speech, whose aid in works we find, 15
And in necessities to mortals kind:

Dire weapon of the tongue, which men revere,
Be present, Hermes, and thy suppliant hear;
Assist my works, conclude my life with peace,
Give graceful speech, and me memory's increase. 20

XXVIII.

TO PROSERPINE.

A HYMN

DAUGHTER of Jove, almighty and divine,
Come, blessed queen, and to these rites incline:
Only-begotten, Pluto's honor'd wife, 3
O venerable Goddess, source of life:
'Tis thine in earth's profundities to dwell, 5
Fast by the wide and dismal gates of hell:
Jove's holy offspring, of a beauteous mien,
Fatal, with lovely locks, infernal queen:
Source of the furies, whose blest frame proceeds
From Jove's ineffable and secret seeds: 10
Mother of Bacchus, Sonorous, divine,
And many-form'd, the parent of the vine:
The dancing Hours attend thee, essence bright,
All-ruling virgin, bearing heav'nly light:

Illustrious, horned, of a bounteous mind, 13
Alone desir'd by those of mortal kind.
O, vernal queen, whom grassy plains delight,
Sweet to the smell, and pleasing to the sight:

Whose holy form in budding fruits we view,
Earth's vig'rous offspring of a various hue: 20
Espous'd in Autumn: life and death alone 21
To wretched mortals from thy power is known:
For thine the task according to thy will, 23
Life to produce, and all that lives to kill.

Hear, blessed Goddess, send a rich increase 25
Of various fruits from earth, with lovely Peace;
Send Health with gentle hand, and crown my life
With blest abundance, free from noisy strife;
Last in extreme old age the prey of Death,
Dismiss we willing to the realms beneath, 30
To thy fair palace, and the blissful plains
Where happy spirits dwell, and Pluto reigns.

Footnotes

3   Ver. 3] *Only-begotten*. Καὶ γὰρ ὁ Θεολογός την κόρην ΜΟΥΝΟ-ΓΕΝΕΙΑΝ ἔιαθε προσαγορεύειν. Proc. Tim. 2 extra p. 139. 9. i.e. "I see that the theologist (meaning Orpheus) calls Proserpine, "Only-begotten".

21   Ver. 21.] *Espous'd in Autumn*. We have already observed in the Dissertation, that the Orphic theologers considered a difference of sex in the divinities; attributing the male to some, and the female to others. Now the mutual commerce and energy subsisting between these Gods and Goddesses, they denominated Ιεροι Γαμοι, i. e. "holy marriages:" or according to Proclus, on the Parmenides of Plato, as cited by Eschenbach, in Epig. p. 59. they mystically called, the simple kindred conjunction, and communion of divine causes, a marriage. And Proserpine, or the animating part of the earth's soul, may he considered as resting in Autumn, from all farther productions; her powers at that time having attained their full perfection.

    Hence at this period may we not say, that she is wholly abstracted from the animal life, and secretly united with Pluto, or the intellectual part of the earth's soul; from whom she receives the divine light of mind, and copious streams of the nectar of divine knowledge.

23 Ver. 23.] *For thine the task*, &c. Proclus, in Theol. Plat. p. 371, informs us, that, according to the Eleusinian mysteries, Proserpine together with Pluto, governs terrestrial concerns, and the recesses of the earth: that she supplies life to the extreme parts of the universe, and imparts soul to those, who, by her power, are rendered inanimate and dead. This is perfectly agreeable to the 23d and following line.

XXIX.

TO BACCHUS.

The FUMIGATION from STORAX.

BACCHUS I call, loud-sounding and divine,
Fanatic God, a two-fold shape is thine:
Thy various names and attributes I sing,
O, first-born, thrice begotten, Bacchic king: 4
Rural, ineffable, two-form'd, obscure, 5
Two-horn'd, with ivy crown'd, euion, pure.
Bull-fac'd, and martial, bearer of the vine,
Endu'd with counsel prudent and divine:
Triennial, whom the leaves of vines adorn,
Of Jove and Proserpine, occultly born. 10

Immortal dæmon, hear my suppliant voice,
Give me in blameless plenty to rejoice;
And listen gracious to my mystic pray'r,
Surrounded with thy choir of nurses fair.

Footnotes

4   Ver. 4.] *O, first-born*. See the notes to Hymn v. to Protogonus.

XXX.

TO THE CURETES.

A HYMN.

LEAPING Curetes, who with dancing feet
And circling measures, armed footsteps beat:
Whose bosom's mad, fanatic transports fire,
Who move in rythm to the founding lyre:
Who traces deaf when lightly leaping tread,
Arm bearers, strong defenders, rulers dread:
Propitious omens, guards of Proserpine *,
Preserving rites, mysterious and divine
Come, and benevolent my words attend,
(In herds rejoicing), and my life defend. 10

Footnotes

*   Proclus calls the Curetes, guards of Proserpine, lib. vi. Theol. Plat. p. 383.

XXXI.

TO PALLAS.

A HYMN.

ONLY-Begotten, noble race of Jove,
Blessed and fierce, who joy'st in caves to rove: 2

O, warlike Pallas, whose illustrious kind,
Ineffable and effable we find:
Magnanimous and fam'd, the rocky height, 5
And groves, and shady mountains thee delight:
In arms rejoicing, who with Furies dire
And wild, the souls of mortals dost inspire.
Gymnastic virgin of terrific mind,
Dire Gorgons bane, unmarried, blessed, kind: 10
Mother of arts, imperious; understood,
Rage to the wicked., wisdom to the good:
Female and male, the arts of war are thine,
Fanatic, much-form'd dragoness, divine: 14
O'er the Phlegrean giants rous'd to ire, 15 15
Thy coursers driving, with destruction dire.

Sprung from the head of Jove, of splendid mien,
Purger of evils, all-victorious queen.

Hear me, O Goddess, when to thee I pray,
With supplicating voice both night and day, 20

And in my latest hour, peace and health,
Propitious times, and necessary wealth,
And, ever present, be thy vot'ries aid,
O, much implor'd, art's parent, blue eyed maid.

Footnotes

2   XXXI. Ver. 2.] *Who joy'st in caves to rove.* Proclus, in Plat. Theol, P. 372. informs us, that there are three zoogonic or vivific monads, Diana, Proserpine, and Minerva; and that these three divinities exist together. Hence the reason is obvious why this Goddess is celebrated as living in caves, and delighting in rocks and mountains, from her agreement with Diana: and hence is appears, that Rutikenius was mistaken in imagining these epithets were misplaced. We may likewise see the reason from hence, why Minerva is called, in line 14, Female and Male, as well as the Moon; and why the Moon is called in the Hymn to her πάνσοφε κύρη, i. e. "all-wife virgin."

14   Ver. 14.] *Much-form'd dragoness.* It is easy to perceive the agreement between Minerva, who is the same with divine Wisdom and Providence, and a Dragon; since according to Phurnutus, a dragon is of a vigilant and guardian nature.

15   Ver. 15.] *O'er the Phlegrean giants*, &c. The fable of the giants is common; but its philosophical explanation is, I fear, but little known and less understood. For the sake of the liberal, therefore, the following account of the battles of the Gods, from the excellent Commentary of Proclus, on Plato's Republic, p. 373, is inserted. "The divisible progressions of all beings, and the diversities of substances, receive a supernal origin, from a division of unknown primitive causes, which are mutually at strife with principles, subject to the universe. For some determine their essence about unity, on which they depend; and others receive in themselves a never-failing power of infinity, by which they generate universals, and a cause of multitude and progression, according to which they possess their peculiar essences. Hence, after the same manner as the first principles of beings, are mutually separated from each other; so all divine genera and true beings have among themselves a

progression distinguished by order. In consequence of this, some insert in things posterior the principle cause of unity; but others afford the power of separation. Some are the causes of conversion to inferiors, and of collecting the multitude of progressive natures to their proper principles: while others promote their progression and procreation, emanating from principles, as their source. Some supply the power of generating to inferiors; and others exhibit a constant and undefiled purity. There are some, again, containing the cause of separable goods; and others, of such goods as subsist together with their recipients. Indeed, after this manner, the various contrariety of such kinds appears in all the administrations of true being. Thus the station or quiet of things constantly establishing being in themselves, resists efficacious and vital powers of motion. So the communication of identity, on every side similar to itself (if the expression may be allowed) is specially opposed to the discretions of diversity. Thus, too, similitude fights with dissimilitude, and equality with inequality. Since this is the case, can it be wonderful, that mythologists, perceiving a contrariety of this kind among the Gods, and the first principles of things, should represent it to their pupils by contentions and wars? For though the divine genera are always united with each other, yet they preside as well over those who administer to union, as over those who machinate confusion. And this is the first reason of the wars of the Gods. But it is lawful to produce another reason, and to affirm that the Gods are indeed indivisibly conjoined, and subsist together in mutual uniformity: but that their progressions into the universe, and participations by recipient natures, become disjoined and divisible, and by this means filled with contrariety. For things subject to the power of the Gods, cannot receive their diffused powers, and multiform illustrations, without mixture and confusion. Hence the last orders dependent on the Gods, since they are produced by a long interval from the first causes, but are contiguous to the concerns they administer, and adhere to matter, contract contrariety, and an all-various division; partially presiding over material affairs, and diminishing and dispersing those separate powers, which before subsisted in a superior manner, uniformly and indivisibly, in their primitive causes. Since, then, such and so many are the ways, by which, according to the mysteries of theologists, war is usually referred to the Gods; other poets who, seized with fury, have interpreted divine concerns, introduced the battles and wars of the Gods, according to the first reasons, i. e. so far as the divine genera admit of diversity, according to the first principles of all things. For fables, concealing truth under a veil, shew that such things as recall to principles, oppose and fight with the authors of generation: collecting with separating natures, things unifying with such as multiply by the progression of beings; and universal genera, with such as operate in a partial and particular manner. Hence they relate, that the Titans (or dæmons subservient to Nature) fight with Bacchus, (or Nature) and the giants with Jove. For union, and an indivisible work, is proper to Bacchus and Jupiter, as the demiurgic causes of the world; but the Titans and Giants produce the demiurgic powers into multitude; partially administering the concerns of the universe, and existing as the proximate parents of material natures." Thus far Proclus. For a farther account of Minerva, see the note to Hymn ix. to Nature.

XXXII.

TO VICTORY.

The FUMIGATION from MANNA.

O Powerful Victory, by men desir'd,
With adverse breasts to dreadful fury fir'd,
Thee I invoke, whose might alone can quell
Contending rage, and molestation fell:
'Tis thine in battle to confer the crown, 5
The victor's prize, the mark of sweet renown;
For thou rul'st all things, Victory divine!
And glorious strife, and joyful shouts are thine.
Come, mighty Goddess, and thy suppliant bless,
With sparkling eye, elated with success; 10
May deeds illustrious thy protection claim,
And find, led on by thee immortal Fame.

XXXIII.

TO APOLLO.

The FUMIGATION from MANNA.

BLEST Pæan, come, propitious to my pray'r,
Illustrious pow'r, whom Memphian tribes revere,
Slayer of Tityus, and the God of health,
Lycorian Phœbus, fruitful source of wealth .
Spermatic, golden-lyr'd, the field from thee 5
Receives it's constant, rich fertility.
Titanic, Grunian, Smynthian, thee I sing, 7
Python-destroying, hallow'd, Delphian king:
Rural, light-bearer, and the Muse's head,
Noble and lovely, arm'd with arrows dread: 10
Far-darting, Bacchian, two-fold, and divine, 11
Pow'r far diffused, and course oblique is thine.
O, Delian king, whose light-producing eye
Views all within, and all beneath the sky:

Whose locks are gold, whose oracles are sure, 15
Who, omens good reveal'st, and precepts pure:
Hear me entreating for the human kind,
Hear, and be present with benignant mind;

For thou survey'st this boundless æther all,
And ev'ry part of this terrestrial ball 20
Abundant, blessed; and thy piercing sight,
Extends beneath the gloomy, silent night;
Beyond the darkness, starry-ey'd, profound,
The stable roots, deep fix'd by thee are found.
The world's wide bounds, all-flourishing are thine, 25
Thyself all the source and end divine:
'Tis thine all Nature's music to inspire,
With various-sounding, harmonising lyre;
Now the last string thou tun'ft to sweet accord, 29
Divinely warbling now the highest chord; 30

Th' immortal golden lyre, now touch'd by thee,
Responsive yields a Dorian melody.

All Nature's tribes to thee their diff'rence owe,
And changing seasons from thy music flow
Hence, mix'd by thee in equal parts, advance 35
Summer and Winter in alternate dance;
This claims the highest, that the lowest string,
The Dorian measure tunes the lovely spring .
Hence by mankind, Pan-royal, two-horn'd nam'd, 39
Emitting whistling winds thro' Syrinx fam'd; 40 40
Since to thy care, the figur'd seal's consign'd, 41
Which stamps the world with forms of ev'ry kind.

Hear me, blest pow'r, and in these rites rejoice,
And save thy mystics with a suppliant voice.

Footnotes

7   Ver. 7.] *Grunian*. According to Strabo, lib. xiii. Grynæus is a town of Myrinæus: likewise, a temple of Apollo, and a most ancient oracle and temple, sumptuously built of white stone. Gyrald. Syntag. p. 237.

11 Ver. 11.] *Far-darting*.ἑκατηβελετησ Proclus, on Plato's Cratylus, informs us he is so called, ὅτι χορηγὸσ ὥς, καὶ εξερομενοσ ἐπὶ παντασ ποιεῖ τας ενεργείας. i. e, "because since he is the choragus or leader of the choir of the Muses, he produces energies in all things."

29 Ver. 29.] *Now the last string*, &c. Gesner well observes, in his notes to this Hymn, that the comparison and conjunction of the musical and astronomical elements are most ancient; being derived from Orpheus and Pythagoras, to Plato. Now, according to the Orphic and Pythagoric doctrine, the lyre of Apollo is an image of the celestial harmony, or the melody caused by the orderly revolutions of the celestial spheres. But I cannot believe that Orpheus and Pythagoras considered this harmony as attended with sensible sounds, according to the vulgar acceptation of the word: for it is surely more rational to suppose, that they meant nothing more by the music of the spheres, than their harmonical proportions to each other. Indeed these wise men, to whom metaphors were familiar, may be easily conceived by vulgar sound and vulgar harmony to insinuate internal sound, and harmony subsisting in its origin and cause. Hence we may consider the souls of the celestial spheres, together with the soul of the world, as composing the choir of the nine Muses; (who are called by the Platonists nine Syrens) and dancing in numerical order round Apollo the sun of the intellectual world. But these nine Muses are far different from the marine Syrens of the poets who, resident as it were in the sea of material delights, draw us aside by their alluring melody, from the paths of rectitude. For these are divine Syrens inviting us to the proper end of our nature; and forming from the eight tones of the eight spheres, one perfect and everlasting harmony.

The following quotation from the Platonic Nichomachus, Harm. i. p. 6. illustrates the meaning of the Hypate and Nete, or the highest and lowest string. From the motion of Saturn, (says he) "The most remote of the planets, the appellation of the gravest sound, Hypate, is derived: but from the lunar motion, which is the lowest of all, the most acute sound is called νεάτη, Nete, or the lowest." But Gesner observes, that a more ancient, and as it were archetypal appellation, is derived from the ancient triangular lyre, a copy of which was found among the pictures lately dug out of the ruins of Herculaneum; where the highest chord next to the chin of the musicians is the longest, and consequently (says he) the sound is the most grave. Gesner proceeds in observing, that the three seasons of the year are so compared together in a musical ratio, that Hypate signifies the Winter, Nete the Summer, and the Dorian measure represents the intermediate seasons, Spring and Autumn. Now the reason why the Dorian melody is assigned to the Spring, is because that measure wholly consists in temperament and moderation, as we learn from Plut. de Mus. p. 1136. E. and consequently is with great propriety attributed to the Spring, considered as placed between Summer and Winter; and gratefully tempering the fervent heat of the one, and the intense cold of the other.

39   Ver. 39.] *Pan-royal.* See the notes to the Hymn to Pan, to Hercules, and the Sun.

40   Ver. 40.] *Emitting whistling winds.* Johannes Diaconus, in Allegorcis Theogoniæ Hesiodi, quotes the following lines from Orpheus.

Ζεὺς δέ τε πάντων ἐςὶ θεὸς, πάντων τε κεραςὴς,

Πνεύμασι συζι#ων, ($συξι:ζαν$) φωναῖσι τε ἀερομικτοις·

That is, "But Jupiter is the God of all, and the mingler of all things; whistling with the breathing winds and aerial voices." And this perfectly agrees with Apollo, considered as Jupiter, or the sun of the intelligible world.

41   Ver. 41.] *The figur'd seal.* Since Apollo in the intelligible world is the demiurgus of the universe, and consequently comprehends in his essence the archetypal ideas of all sensible forms, he may with great propriety be said to posses the figured seal, of which every visible species is nothing more than an impression. It is however necessary to observe, that in the great seal of ideas, all forms subsist in indivisible union and immaterial perfection: but in their imitative impressions in bodies, they are found full of boundless multitude, and material imperfection.

XXXIV.

TO LATONA.

The FUMIGATION from MYRRH.

DARK veil'd Latona, much invoked queen,
Twin-bearing Goddess, of a noble mien;
Cæantis great, a mighty mind is thine,
Offspring prolific, blest of Jove divine:
Phœbus proceeds from thee, the God of light, 5
And Dian fair, whom winged darts delight;
She in Ortygia's honor'd regions born,
In Delos he, which mountains high adorn.
Hear me, O Goddess, with propitious mind,
And end these holy rites, with aspect kind. 10

XXXV.

TO DIANA.

The FUMIGATION from MANNA.

Hear me, Jove's daughter, celebrated queen,
Bacchian and Titan, of a noble mien:

In darts rejoicing and on all to shine,
Torch-bearing Goddess, Dictynna divine;
O'er births presiding, and thyself a maid, 5
To labour-pangs imparting ready aid:
Dissolver of the zone and wrinkl'd care,
Fierce huntress, glorying in the Sylvan war:
Swift in the course, in dreadful arrows skill'd,
Wandering by night, rejoicing in the field: 10
Of manly form, erect, of bounteous mind,
Illustrious dæmon, nurse of human kind:
Immortal, earthly, bane of monsters fell,
'Tis thine; blest maid, on woody hills to dwell:
Foe of the stag, whom woods and dogs delight, 15
In endless youth who flourish fair and bright.
O, universal queen, august, divine,
A various form, Cydonian pow'r, is thine:

Dread guardian Goddess, with benignant mind
Auspicious, come to mystic rites inclin'd 20
Give earth a store of beauteous fruits to bear,
Send gentle Peace, and Health with lovely hair,
And to the mountains drive Disease and Care.

Footnotes

5 Ver. 5.] *O'er births presiding.* In the original, λοχεία: and Proclus, in Plat. Theol. p. 403. observes that this epithet is given to Diana by theologians, because she is the inspector of natural progression and generation.

XXXVI.

TO THE TITANS *

The FUMIGATION from FRANKINCENSE.

O Mighty Titans, who from heav'n and earth
Derive your noble and illustrious birth,
Our fathers fires, in Tartarus profound
Who dwell, deep merg'd beneath the solid ground:
Fountains and principles, from whom began 5
Th' afflicted, miserable, race of man:
Who not alone in earth's retreats abide,
But in the ocean and the air reside;
Since ev'ry species from your nature flows,
Which all prolific, nothing barren knows: 10
Avert your rage, if from th' infernal seats
One of your tribe should visit our retreats.

Footnotes

*   See note to Hymn xxxi. to Pallas.

XXXVII.

TO THE CURETES +.

The FUMIGATION from FRANKINCENSE.

Brass-beating Salians, ministers of Mars,
Who guard his arms the instruments of wars
Whose blessed frames, heav'n, earth, and sea compose,
And from whose breath all animals arose:
Who dwell in Samothracia's sacred ground, 5
Defending mortals thro' the sea profound.
Deathless Curetes, by your pow'r alone,
Initial rites to men at first were shewn:
Who shake old Ocean thund'ring to the sky,
And stubborn oaks with branches waving high. 10
'Tis your's in glittering arms the earth to beat,
With lightly-leaping, rapid, sounding feet;
Then every beast the noise terrific flies,
And the loud tumult wanders thro' the skies:
The dust your feet excites with matchless force, 15
Flies to the clouds amidst their whirling course;
And ev'ry flower of variegated hue,
Grows in the dancing motion form'd by you.
Immortal dæmons, to your pow'rs consign'd
The talk to nourish, and destroy mankind. 20

When rushing furious with loud tumult dire,
O'erwhelm'd, they perish in your dreadful ire;
And live replenish'd with the balmy air,
The food of life, committed to your care.
When shook by you, the seas, with wild uproar, 25
Wide-spreading, and profoundly whirling, roar:
The concave heav'ns, with Echo's voice resound,
When leaves with ruffling noise bestrew the ground.
Curetes, Corybantes, ruling kings,
Whose praise the land of Samothracia sings: 30
From Jove descended; whose immortal breath
Sustains the soul, and wafts her back from death;
Aerial-form'd, much-fam'd, in heav'n ye shine
Two-fold, in heav'n all-lucid and divine:
Blowing, serene, from whom abundance springs, 35
Nurses of seasons, fruit-producing kings.

Footnotes

+ XXXVII. + The Curetes are plainly celebrated in this Hymn as the winds; the reason of which is as follows. Saturn, who according to the Orphic theology as related by Proclus, is allotted a supercelestial and intellectual essence produced Jupiter from Rhea. And Jupiter, or the demiurgus of the universe, silently emerged into light from the three principles, Æther, Chaos, and Night conflicting together, and mutually concurring with, and separating from each other. Now these three principles are interpreted by Julian, Orat. v. as the Corybantes: and hence with perfect agreement to the Orphic symbolical theology, the mutual conflict of these principles, is represented by the impetuous Fury of the winds.

XXXVIII.

TO CORYBAS *

The FUMIGATION from FRANKINCENSE.

THE mighty ruler of this earthly ball,
For ever flowing, to these rites I call;

Martial and blest, unseen by mortal sight,
Preventing fears, and pleas'd with gloomy night:
Hence, fancy's terrors are by thee allay'd, 5
All-various king, who lov'st the desart shade:
Each of thy brothers killing, blood is thine,
Two-fold Curete, many-form'd, divine.
By thee transmuted Ceres' body pure,
Became a dragon's savage and obscure: 10
Avert thy anger, hear me when I pray,
And by fix'd fate, drive fancy's fears away.

Footnotes

*   The following curious passage is preserved to us by Athenagoras, in Legat. i. pro Christianis; in which Orpheus describes the generation of the celestial or intellectual earth, "But Phanes or Protogonus, produced another dire offspring from his holy womb; the dreadful form of a dragon. It has hairs on its head, and a beautiful countenance, but the rest of its body is that of a dragon, tremendous to the view." Now from this passage I conclude that Corybas, in the present Hymn, is the same with Protogonus: for he is celebrated, v. 9, 10. as changing by his arts, the holy body of Ceres (or the earth) into the form of a savage and obscure dragon. And as in the above lines the intellectual earth is represented under the form of a dragon with a beautiful countenance; the sensible earth, which is but the image of the intellectual, may with perfect agreement to this fragment be called an obscure dragon, since obscurity is an apt symbol of a material nature.

Corybas is likewise said, v. 7. to kill his two brothers. Now since Corybas is Protogonus, his two brothers may be considered as Æther and Chaos, whose occult union formed the achytypal egg of the universe: and Protogonus bursting forth from this egg, and by this means dispersing Æther and Chaos, may be aptly represented under the symbol of Corybas destroying his two brothers. For, according to Proclus, it is customary with divine poets, to imitate the exalted powers of exemplars, by contrary and most remote adumbrations.

XXXIX.

TO CERES.

The FUMIGATION from STORAX.

O Universal mother, Ceres fam'd
August, the source of wealth, and various nam'd: 2
Great nurse, all-bounteous, blessed and divine,
Who joy'st in peace, to nourish corn is thine:
Goddess of seed, of fruits abundant, fair, 5
Harvest and threshing, are thy constant care;
Who dwell'st in Eleusina's seats retir'd,
Lovely, delightful queen, by all desir'd.
Nurse of all mortals, whose benignant mind,
First ploughing oxen to the yoke confin'd; 10
And gave to men, what nature's wants require,
With plenteous means of bliss which all desire.
In verdure flourishing in honor bright,
Assessor of great Bacchus, bearing light:

Rejoicing in the reapers sickles, kind, 15
Whose nature lucid, earthly, pure, we find.
Prolific, venerable, Nurse divine,
Thy daughter loving, holy Proserpine:

A car with dragons yok'd, 'tis thine to guide, 19
And orgies singing round thy throne to ride: 20
Only-begotten, much-producing queen,
All flowers are thine and fruits of lovely green.
Bright Goddess, come, with Summer's rich increase
Swelling and pregnant, leading smiling Peace;
Come, with fair Concord and imperial Health, 25
And join with these a needful store of wealth.

Footnotes

2   Ver. 2.] The source of wealth. The following Orphic verse is preserved to us by Diodorus Siculus, i. 32,. which perfectly agrees with the present Hymn.

Γῆ μήτηρ πάντων, Δημήτηρ, πλυτοδότειρα.

That is, "Earth, mother of all things, Ceres, source of wealth."

19 Ver. 19.] *A car with dragons yok'd.* Since, according to our notes on the preceding Hymn to Corybas, Ceres, or the Earth, is represented by Orpheus under the form of an obscure dragon, it is not wonderful that she should be drawn by dragons.

XL.

TO THE CERALIAN MOTHER.

The FUMIGATION from AROMATICS.

CERALIAN queen, of celebrated name,
From whom both men, and Gods immortal came;
Who widely wand'ring once, oppress'd with grief,
In Eleusina's valley found'st relief,
Discovering Proserpine thy daughter pure 5
In dread Avernus, dismal and obscure;
A sacred youth while thro' the world you stray
Bacchus, attending leader of the way;
The holy marriage of terrestrial Jove
Relating, while oppress'd with grief you rove; 10
Come, much invok'd, and to these rites inclin'd,
Thy mystic suppliant bless, with fav'ring mind.

XLI.

TO MISES.

The FUMIGATION from STORAX.

Call Thesmophorus *, spermatic God,
Of various names, who bears the leafy rod:
Mises, ineffable, pure, sacred queen,
Two-fold Iacchus, male and female seen:
Illustr'ous, whether to rejoice is thine
In incense offer'd, in the fane divine +;
Or if in Phrygia most thy soul delights,
Performing with thy mother sacred rites;
Or if the land of Cyprus is thy care,
Well pleas'd to dwell with Cytherea fair; 10

Or if exulting in the fertile plains
With thy dark mother Isis, where she reigns, 12
With nurses pure attended, near the flood
Of sacred Egypt, thy divine abode:

Wherever resident, blest pow'r attend, 15
And with benignant mind these labours end.

Footnotes

* Or the legislator.

+ Or Eleusina.

12 *My dark mother Isis.* According to Plutarch, in his treatise of Isis and Osiris, Isis is the mother of Orus, who is called by the Greeks Apollo; and Iacchus it is well known is a mythic sirname of Bacchus. Now Apollo is frequently called in the orphic writings Bacchus; as in the Hymn to that deity, *Bacchian and Two-fold*. And Apollo, as we have frequently observed, is in the intelligible world, the king and father of the universe, Protogonus, or Ericapæus, and in the sensible world the Sun. So that Mises or Bacchus is celebrated in this Hymn by the same appellations as are given to Protogonus and Apollo: for he is called spermatic, ineffable, male and female, &c. which last appellation is given to Protogonus in the Orphic verse preserved by Proclus, lib. ii. in Timæum.

Θή#ισ καὶ γενέτωρ κρατερὸς θεὸς ἠρικεπαῖοσ

That is, "Female and father (or male), strong God Ericapæus"

Indeed it is common with the Orphic theologers, to celebrate causes as the same with effects, and effects with their causes; the supreme as the subordinate, and the subordinate as the supreme. And this in consequence of the mysterious union, subsisting between all the divine orders, and through every part of the universe; every thing, except the first cause, being stamped as it were with the same great seals of ideas, and existing on this account in sympathy and similitude with natures, both superior and subordinate to its essence. And here I cannot but take notice of the mistake of Macrobius, who imagines that all the Gods according to Orpheus, may be reduced to the Sun; the other divinities being but so many different appellations of that deity: for it is sufficiently evident to those who are skilled in the Orphic theology, that Orpheus was a Polytheist as well as a monarchist. But this mistake of Macrobius is not wonderful; as we may say of him what Plotinus said, on reading the book of Longinus *concerning principles*, φιλόλογοσ μὲν ὁ Λογγῖνοσ, φιλόσοφοσ δὲ ὑδαμῶσ, i. e. "Longinus is a philologist, but by no means a philosopher." Similar to this is the mistake of modern Mythologists, who in conformity with the fashionable philosophy, call the material parts of nature, the Gods of the ancients: the folly and impiety of which system, cannot be better represented than in the words of Plutarch in his above mentioned curious Treatise of Isis and Osiris, which I shall give the reader in the elegant Translation of Dr. Squire, p. 90. "We ought to take the greatest care (says Plutarch) that we do not explain away the very nature of the Gods, by resolving it as it were into mere blasts of wind, or streams of rivers, into the sowing and earing of corn, or into the changes of the earth and seasons, as those persons have actually done, who make Bacchus to be Wine, and Vulcan Fire. Just as Cleanthes somewhere tells us, that by Proserpine nothing else is meant, but that air which pervading the fruits of the earth, is thereby destroyed as it were, being deprived of its nutritive spirit and as a certain poet, speaking of reaping corn, says,

Then, when the vigorous youth shall Ceres cut.

For those who indulge themselves in this manner of expression, act just as wisely as they would do, who should call the sails, the cables, and the anchors of the ship, the pilot; or the yarn and web, the weaver; or the emulsion, the easing draught, and the ptifan, the physician. "And, p. 91. he observes, that as the sun and the moon, and the heavens, and the earth, and the sea, though common to all mankind, have different names given them by different people; so may the same be affirmed, likewise, of that one supreme reason, who framed this world, and of that one providence which governs and watches over the whole, and of those *subordinate ministring powers that are set over the universe*, that they are the very same everywhere, though the honors which are paid them, as well as the appellations which are given them, are different in different places, according to the laws of each country, as are likewise those symbols, under which the mystics endeavour to lead their votaries to the knowledge of divine truths: and though some of these are more clear and explicit than others, yet are they not any of them without hazard; for whilst some persons, by wholly mistaking their meaning and appellation, have thereby plunged themselves into *superstition*, others, that they might avoid so fatal a quagmire, are unawares, dashed themselves upon the rock of *atheism*."

XLII

TO THE SEASONS.

The FUMIGATION from AROMATICS.

DAUGHTERS of Jove and Themis, seasons bright,
Justice, and blessed peace, and lawful right,
Vernal and grassy, vivid, holy pow'rs,
Whose balmy breath exhales in lovely flow'rs
All-colour'd seasons, rich increase your care, 5
Circling, for ever flourishing and fair:
Invested with a veil of shining dew,
A flow'ry veil delightful to the view:

Attending Proserpine, when back from night,
The Fates and Graces lead her up to light; 10
When in a band-harmonious they advance,
And joyful round her, form the solemn dance:
With Ceres triumphing, and Jove divine;
Propitious come, and on our incense shine;
Give earth a blameless store of fruits to bear, 15
And make a novel mystic's life your care.

XLIII.

TO SEMELE.

The FUMIGATION from STORAX.

CADMEAN Goddess, universal queen,
Thee, Semele I call, of beauteous mien;
Deep-bosom'd, lovely flowing locks are thine,
Mother of Bacchus, joyful and divine,
The mighty offspring, whom love's thunder bright, 5
Forc'd immature, and fright'ned into light:
Born from the deathless counsels, secret, high,
Of Jove Saturnian, regent of the sky
Whom Proserpine permits to view the light,
And visit mortals from the realms of night: 10
Constant attending on the sacred rites,
And feast triennial, which thy soul delights;
When thy son's wond'rous birth mankind relate,
And secrets deep, and holy celebrate.

Now I invoke thee, great Cadmean queen, 15
To bless these rites with countenance serene.

XLIV.

TO DIONYSIUS BASSAREUS TRIENNALIS [*].

A HYMN

COME, blessed Dionysius, various nam'd,
Bull-fac'd, begot from Thunder, Bacchus fam'd.
Bassarian God, of universal might,
Whom swords, and blood, and sacred rage delight:
In heav'n rejoicing, mad, loud-sounding God, 5
Furious inspirer, bearer of the rod:
By Gods rever'd, who dwell'st with human kind,
Propitious come, with much-rejoicing mind.

Footnotes

[*] So called because his rites were performed every third year.

XLV.

TO LIKNITUS + BACCHUS.

The FUMIGATION from MANNA.

LIKNITAN Bacchus, bearer of the vine,
Thee I invoke to bless these rites divine:

Florid and gay, of nymphs the blossom bright,
And of fair Venus, Goddess of delight,
'Tis thine mad footsteps with mad nymphs to beat, 5
Dancing thro' groves with lightly leaping feet:
From Jove's high counsels nurst by Proserpine,
And born the dread of all the pow'rs divine:
Come, blessed pow'r, regard thy suppliant's voice,
Propitious come, and in these rites rejoice. 10

Footnotes

+ XLV. + Or the Fan-bearer.
　　Concerning Liknitus and the following Bacchuses, see the last section of the Dissertation.

XLVI.

TO BACCHUS PERICIONIUS *.

The FUMIGATION from AROMATICS.

BACCHUS Pericionius, hear my pray'r,
Who mad'st the house of Cadmus once thy care,
With matchless force, his pillars twining round,
(When burning thunders shook the solid ground,
In flaming, founding torrents borne along), 5
Propt by thy grasp indissolubly strong.
Come mighty Bacchus to these rites inclin'd,
And bless thy suppliants with rejoicing mind.

Footnotes

* So called from περι and κιονισ, a little pillar.

XLVII.

TO SABASIUS.

The FUMIGATION from AROMATICS

HEAR me, illustrious father, dæmon fam'd.
Great Saturn's offspring, and Sabasius nam'd;

Inserting Bacchus, bearer of the vine,
And founding God, within thy thigh divine,
That when mature, the Dionysian God 5
Might burst the bands of his conceal'd abode,
And come to sacred Tmolus, his delight,
Where Ippa dwells, all beautiful and bright.
Come blessed Phrygian God, the king of all,
And aid thy mystics, when on thee they call. 10

XLVIII.

TO IPPA *

The FUMIGATION from STORAX.

Great nurse of Bacchus, to my pray'r incline,
For holy Sabus' secret rites are thine,
The mystic rites of Bacchus' nightly choirs,
Compos'd of sacred, loud-resounding fires:
Hear me, terrestrial mother, mighty queen, 5
Whether on Phyrgia's holy mountain + seen,
Or if to dwell in Tmolus thee delights,
With holy aspect come, and bless these rites.

Footnotes

* Ippa according to Proclus is same with Juno.
+ Ida.

XLIX.

TO LYSIUS LENÆUS.

A HYMN.

Hear me, Jove's son, blest Bacchus, God of wine,
Born of two mothers, honor'd and divine;
Lysian, Euion * Bacchus, various-nam'd,
Of Gods the offspring secret, holy, fam'd:
Fertile and nourishing whose liberal care 5
Earth's fruits increases, flourishing and fair;
Sounding, magnanimous, Lenæan pow'r
O various form'd, medic'nal, holy flow'r:
Mortals in thee, repose from labour find,
Delightful charm, desir'd by all mankind: 10
Fair-hair'd Euion, Bromian, joyful God,
Lysian, invested with the leafy rod.
To these our rites, benignant pow'r incline,
When fav'ring men, or when on Gods you shine;
Be present to thy mystic's suppliant pray'r, 15
Rejoicing come, and fruits abundant bear.

Footnotes

*   Euion ingeminat, reparabilis assonat Echo. *Persius*.

L.

TO THE NYMPHS.

The FUMIGATION from AROMATICS.

NYMPHS, who from Ocean's stream derive your birth,
Who dwell in liquid caverns of the earth

Nurses of Bacchus secret-coursing pow'r,
Who fruits sustain, and nourish ev'ry flow'r:
Earthly, rejoicing, who in meadows dwell, 5
And caves and dens, whose depths extend to hell:
Holy, oblique, who swiftly soar thro' air,
Fountains and dews, and mazy streams your care:
Seen and unseen, who joy with wand'rings wide
And gentle course, thro' flow'ry vales to glide; 10
With Pan exulting on the mountains height,
Loud-founding, mad, whom rocks and woods delight:
Nymphs od'rous, rob'd in white, whose streams exhale
The breeze refreshing, and the balmy gale;
With goats and pastures pleas'd, and beasts of prey, 15
Nurses of fruits, unconscious of decay:
In cold rejoicing, and to cattle kind,
Sportive thro' ocean wand'ring unconfin'd:

Nysian, fanatic Nymphs, whom oaks delight,
Lovers of Spring, Pæonian virgins bright. 20
With Bacchus, and with Ceres, hear my pray'r.
And to mankind abundant favour bear;
Propitious listen to your suppliants voice,
Come, and benignant in these rites rejoice;
Give plenteous Seasons, and sufficient wealth, 25
And pour; in lasting streams, continued Health.

LI.

TO TRIETERICUS.

The FUMIGATION from AROMATICS.

BACCHUS fanatic, much-nam'd, blest, divine,
Bull-fac'd Lenæan, bearer of the vine;
From fire descended, raging, Nysian king,
From whom initial ceremonies spring:
Liknitan Bacchus, pure and fiery bright, 5
Prudent, crown-bearer, wandering in the night;
Pupil of Proserpine, mysterious pow'r,
Triple, ineffable, Jove's secret flow'r:
Ericapæus, first-begotten nam'd,
Of Gods the father, and the offspring fam'd: 10
Bearing a sceptre, leader of the choir,
Whose dancing feet, fanatic Furies fire,
When the triennial band thou dost inspire.
Loud-sounding, Tages, of a fiery light,
Born of two mothers, Amphietus bright: 15

Wand'ring on mountains, cloth'd with skins of deer,
Apollo, golden-ray'd, whom all revere.
God of the grape with leaves of ivy crown'd,

Bassarian, lovely, virgin-like, renown'd
Come blessed pow'r, regard thy mystics voice, 10
Propitious come, and in these rites rejoice.

Footnotes

10   Ver. 10.] *Of Gods the father*, &c. *According* to the fragment preserved by Ficinus, and translated in our Dissertation, Trietericus is the nostic power, or intellect of the Sun; and the Sun is in the sensible world, what Protogonus or Phanes is in the intelligible world, or, in other words, the Sun is the Phanes of the material world, for Trietericus is expressly called in this Hymn Protogonus. With perfect agreement, therefore, to the Orphic theology, Protogonus, considered as the first of the secret genera of the Gods, is the father of the Gods; but considered as the Sun of the material world, he is the offspring of the Gods.

LII.

To AMPHIETUS BACCHUS.

The FUMIGATION from every AROMATIC except FRANKINCENSE.

TERRESTRIAL Dionysius, hear my pray'r,
Awak'ned rise with nymphs of lovely hair:
Great Amphietus Bacchus, annual God,
Who laid asleep in Proserpine's abode,
Did'st lull to drowsy and oblivious rest,
The rites triennial, and the sacred feast;
Which rous'd again by thee, in graceful ring,
Thy nurses round thee mystic anthems sing;
When briskly dancing with rejoicing pow'rs,
Thou mov'st in concert with the circling hours. 10
Come, blessed, fruitful, horned, and divine,
And on these rites with joyful aspect shine;
Accept the general incense and the pray'r,
And make prolific holy fruits thy care.

LIII.

To SILENUS, SATYRUS, and the PRIESTESSES of BACCHUS.

The FUMIGATION from MANNA.

GREAT nurse of Bacchus, to my pray'r incline.,
Silenus, honor'd by the pow'rs divine
And by mankind at the triennial feast
Illustrious dæmon, reverenc'd as the best:
Holy, august, the source of lawful rites, 5
Rejoicing pow'r, whom vigilance delights
With Sylvans dancing ever young and fair,
Head of the Bacchic Nymphs, who ivy bear.
With all thy Satyrs on our incense shine,
Dæmons wild form'd, and bless the rites divine; 10
Come, rouse to sacred Joy thy pupil kin, *
And Brumal Nymphs with rites Lenæan bring;
Our orgies shining thro' the night inspire,
And bless triumphant pow'r the sacred choir.

Footnotes

* Because he was the nurse of Bacchus.

LIV.

TO VENUS.

A HYMN.

HEAV'NLY, illustrious, laughter-loving queen,
Sea-born, night-loving, of an awful mien;

Crafty, from whom necessity first came,
Producing, nightly, all-connecting dame:
'Tis thine the world with harmony to join, 5
For all things spring from thee, O pow'r divine.
The triple Fates are rul'd by thy decree,
And all productions yield alike to thee:
Whate'er the heav'ns, encircling all contain,
Earth fruit-producing, and the stormy main, 10
Thy sway confesses, and obeys thy nod,
Awful attendant of the brumal God:
Goddess of marriage, charming to the sight,
Mother of Loves, whom banquetings delight;
Source of persuasion, secret, fav'ring queen, 15
Illustrious born, apparent and unseen:
Spousal, lupercal, and to men inclin'd,
Prolific, most-desir'd, life-giving., kind:

Great sceptre-bearer of the Gods, 'tis thine,
Mortals in necessary bands to join; 20
And ev'ry tribe of savage monsters dire
In magic chains to bind, thro' mad desire.

Come, Cyprus-born, and to my pray'r incline,
Whether exalted in the heav'ns you shine,
Or pleas'd in Syria's temple to preside, 25
Or o'er th' Egyptian plains thy car to guide,
Fashion'd of gold; and near its sacred flood,
Fertile and fam'd to fix thy blest abode;
Or if rejoicing in the azure shores,
Near where the sea with foaming billows roars, 30
The circling choirs of mortals, thy delight,
Or beauteous nymphs, with eyes cerulean bright,
Pleas'd by the dusty banks renown'd of old,
To drive thy rapid, two-yok'd car of gold;
Or if in Cyprus with thy mother fair, 35
Where married females praise thee ev'ry year,
And beauteous virgins in the chorus join,
Adonis pure to sing and thee divine;
Come, all-attractive to my pray'r inclin'd,
For thee, I call, with holy, reverent mind. 40

Footnotes

5   Ver, 5.] *'Tis thine the world with harmony to join.* According to the Orphic theology as related by Proclus, and from him by Eschenbach, in Epig. p. 52. Venus is the cause of all the harmony and analogy in the universe, and of the union of form with matter; connecting and comprehending the powers of all the mundane elements. And although this Goddess ranks among the supermundane divinities; yet her principal employment consists, in beautifully illuminating the order, harmony, and communion of all mundane concerns.

LV.

TO ADONIS.

The FUMIGATION from AROMATICS.

MUCH-nam'd, and best of dæmons, hear my pray'r,
The desart-loving, deck'd with tender hair;
Joy to diffuse, by all desir'd is thine,
Much form'd, Eubulus; aliment divine
Female and Male, all charming to the sight, 5
Adonis ever flourishing and bright;
At stated periods doom'd to set and rise,
With splendid lamp, the glory of the skies. 8
Two-horn'd and lovely, reverenc'd with tears,
Of beauteous form, adorn'd with copious hairs. 10
Rejoicing in the chace, all-graceful pow'r,
Sweet plant of Venus, Love's delightful flow'r:
Descended from the secret bed divine,
Of lovely-hair'd, infernal Proserpine.
'Tis thine to fink in Tartarus profound, 15
And shine again thro' heav'ns illustrious round,
With beauteous temp'ral orb restor'd to sight;
Come, with earth's fruits, and in these flames delight.

Footnotes

8 Ver. 8.] *With splendid lamp*, &c. Proclus, in his elegant Hymn to the Sun, celebrates him as frequently called Adonis; and this perfectly agrees with the present epithet, and with many others in the Hymn.

LVI.

TO THE TERRESTRIAL HERMES.

The FUMIGATION from STORAX.

HERMES I call, whom Fate decrees to dwell
In the dire path which leads to deepest hell
O Bacchic Hermes, progeny divine
Of Dionysius, parent of the vine,
And of celestial Venus Paphian queen, 5
Dark eye-lash'd Goddess of a lovely mien:
Who constant wand'rest thro' the sacred feats
Where hell's dread empress, Proserpine, retreats;
To wretched souls the leader of thc way
When Fate decrees, to regions void of day: 10
Thine is the wand which causes sleep to fly,
Or lulls to slumb'rous rest the weary eye;
For Proserpine thro' Tart'rus dark and wide
Gave thee forever flowing souls to guide.
Come, blessed pow'r the sacrifice attend, 15
And grant our mystic works a happy end.

LVII.

TO CUPID, OR LOVE.

The FUMIGATION from AROMATICS.

I Call great Cupid, source of sweet delight,
Holy and pure, and lovely to the sight;
Darting, and wing'd, impetuous fierce desire,
With Gods and mortals playing, wand'ring fire:
Cautious, and two-fold, keeper of the keys 5
Of heav'n and earth, the air, and spreading seas;
Of all that Ceres' fertile realms contains,
By which th' all-parent Goddess life sustains,
Or dismal Tartarus is doom'd to keep,
Widely extended, or the sounding, deep; 10

For thee, all Nature's various realms obey,
Who rul'st alone, with universal sway.
Come, blessed pow'r, regard these mystic fires,
And far avert, unlawful mad desires.

LVIII.

TO THE FATES.

The FUMIGATION from AROMATICS.

DAUGHTERS of darkling night, much-nam'd, draw near
Infinite Fates, and listen to my pray'r;
Who in the heav'nly lake (where waters white 3
Burst from a fountain hid in depths of night,
And thro' a dark and stony cavern glide, 5
A cave profound, invisible) abide;

From whence, wide coursing round the boundless earth,
Your pow'r extends to those of mortal birth
To men with hope elated, trifling, gay,
A race presumptuous, born but to decay; 10
Whose life 'tis your's in darkness to conceal
To sense impervious, in a purple veil,
When thro' the fatal plain they joyful ride
In one great car, Opinion for their guide;
'Till each completes his heav'n-appointed round 15
At Justice, Hope, and Care's concluding bound,
The terms absolv'd, prescrib'd by ancient law
Of pow'r immense, and just without a flaw;

For Fate alone with vision unconfin'd,
Surveys the conduct of the mortal kind. 20
Fate is Jove's perfect and eternal eye,
For Jove and Fate our ev'ry deed descry.
Come, gentle pow'rs, well born, benignant, fam'd,
Atropos, Lachesis, and Clotho nam'd:
Unchang'd, aerial, wand'ring in the night, 25
Restless, invisible to mortal fight;
Fates all-producing all-destroying hear,
Regard the incense and the holy pray'r;
Propitious listen to these rites inclin'd,
And far avert distress with placid mind. 30

Footnotes

3   Ver. 3.] *Who in the heav'nly lake*, &c. Gesner confesses he is ignorant what the poet means by the λίμνη Ουρανία, or heavenly lake; as likewise of the dark cavern in which he places the Fates. At first sight indeed the whole seems impenetrably obscure, but on comparing this Hymn with the 68th, to the Furies, we shall find that the poet expressly calls them the Fates; and places them in an obscure cavern by the holy water of Styx. And from hence it appears, that the Heavenly Lake is the same with the Stygian Pool; which is called heavenly perhaps, because the Gods swear by it. But it is not wonderful that the water is called white; since Hesiod, in Theog. v. 791. speaks of the Stygian waters as falling into the sea with silvery whirls. And what strengthens the illustration full more, Fulgentius places the Fates with Pluto.

LIX.

TO THE GRACES.

The FUMIGATION from STORAX.

HEAR me, illustrious Graces, mighty nam'd,
From Jove descended and Eunomia fam'd;
Thalia, and Aglaia fair and bright,
And blest Euphrosyne whom joys delight:
Mothers of mirth, all lovely to the view, 5
Pleasure abundant pure belongs to you:
Various, forever flourishing and fair,
Desir'd by mortals, much invok'd in pray'r:
Circling, dark-ey'd, delightful to mankind,
Come, and your mystics bless with bounteous mind.

LX.

TO NEMESIS.

A HYMN.

THEE, Nemesis I call, almighty queen,
By whom the deeds of mortal life are seen:
Eternal, much rever'd, of boundless sight,
Alone rejoicing in the just and right:
Changing the counsels of the human breast 5
For ever various, rolling without rest.

To every mortal is thy influence known,
And men beneath thy righteous bondage groan;
For ev'ry thought within the mind conceal'd
Is to thy fight perspicuously reveal'd. 10
The soul unwilling reason to obey
By lawless passion rul'd, thy eyes survey.
All to see, hear, and rule, O pow'r divine
Whose nature Equity contains, is thine.
Come, blessed, holy Goddess, hear my pray'r, 15
And make thy mystic's life, thy constant care:
Give aid benignant in the needful hour,
And strength abundant to the reas'ning pow'r;

And far avert the dire, unfriendly race
Of counsels impious, arrogant, and base. 20

LXI.

TO JUSTICE.

The FUMIGATION from FRANKINCENSE.

THE piercing eye of Justice bright, I sing, 1
Plac'd by the throne of heav'n's almighty king,
Perceiving thence, with vision unconfin'd,
The life and conduct of the human kind
To thee, revenge and punishment belong, 5
Chastising ev'ry deed, unjust and wrong;
Whose pow'r alone, dissimilars can join,
And from th' equality of truth combine:
For all the ill, persuasion can inspire,
When urging bad designs, with counsel dire, 10
'Tis thine alone to punish; with the race
Of lawless passions, and incentives base;
For thou art ever to the good inclin'd,
And hostile to the men of evil mind.
Come, all-propitious, and thy suppliant hear, 15
When Fate's predestin'd, final hour draws near.

Footnotes

1 Ver. i.] *The piercing eye.* &c. This Hymn is cited by Demosthenes in his first speech against Aristogiton, as follows: "Let us, says the orator overlooking all custom, judge righteous judgment; let us reverence Eunomia that loves equity, and preserves states; and inexorable Δικη right or justice whom Orpheus our instructor, in the most holy initiations, τελεται, places by the throne of Jove, inspecting the affairs of men. Let each of us imagine her piercing eye is now upon us, and think and vote so as not to dishonour *her* from whom every judge has his name."

LXII.

TO EQUITY.

The FUMIGATION from FRANKINCENSE.

O Blessed Equity, mankind's delight,
Th' eternal friend of conduct just and right:
Abundant, venerable, honor'd maid,
To judgments pure, dispensing constant aid,
A stable conscience, and an upright mind;
For men unjust, by thee are undermin'd,
Whose souls perverse thy bondage ne'er desire,
But more untam'd decline thy scourges dire:
Harmonious, friendly power, averse to strife,
In peace rejoicing, and a stable life; 10
Lovely, loquacious, of a gentle mind,
Hating excess, to equal deeds inclin'd:
Wisdom, and virtue of whate'er degree,
Receive their proper bound alone in thee.
Hear, Goddess Equity, the deeds destroy 15
Of evil men, which human life annoy;
That all may yield to thee of mortal birth,
Whether supported by the fruits of earth,
Or in her kindly fertile bosom found,
or in the depths of Marine Jove profound. 20

LXIII.

TO LAW

A HYMN.

THE holy king of Gods and men I call,
Celestial Law, the righteous seal of all;
The seal which stamps whate'er the earth contains,
Nature's firm basis, and the liquid plains:
Stable, and starry, of harmonious frame, 5
Preserving laws eternally the same:

Thy all-composing pow'r in heaven appears,
Connects its frame, and props the starry spheres;
And shakes weak Envy with tremendous sound,
Toss'd by thy arm in giddy whirls around. 10
'Tis thine, the life of mortals to defend,
And crown existence with a blessed end;
For thy command and alone, of all that lives
Order and rule to ev'ry dwelling gives:
Ever observant of the upright mind, 15
And of just actions the companion kind;
Foe to the lawless, with avenging ire,
Their steps involving in destruction dire.

Come, bless, abundant pow'r, whom all revere,
By all desir'd, with favr'ing mind draw near; 20
Give me thro' life, on thee to fix my fight,
And ne'er forsake the equal paths of right.

LXIV.

TO MARS *.

The FUMIGATION from FRANKINCENSE.

Magnanimous, unconquer'd, boistrous Mars,
In darts rejoicing, and in bloody wars
Fierce and untam'd, whose mighty pow'r can make
The strongest walls from their foundations shake:
Mortal destroying king, defil'd with gore, 5
Pleas'd with war's dreadful and tumultuous roar:
Thee, human blood, and swords, and spears delight,
And the dire ruin of mad savage fight.
Stay, furious contests, and avenging strife,
Whose works with woe, embitter human life; 10
To lovely Venus, and to Bacchus yield,
To Ceres give the weapons of the field;
Encourage peace, to gentle works inclin'd,
And give abundance, with benignant mind.

Footnotes

* This deity, according to Proclus, in Repub. p. 388. perpetually discerns and nourishes, and constantly excites the contrarieties of the universe, that the world may exist perfect and entire from its parts. But he requires the assistance of Venus, that he may insert order and harmony into things contrary and discordant.

LXV.

TO VULCAN *

The FUMIGATION from FRANKINCENSE and MANNA.

STRONG, mighty Vulcan, bearing splendid light,
Unweary'd fire, with flaming torrents bright:
Strong-handed, deathless, and of art divine,
Pure element, a portion of the world is thine:

All-taming artist, all-diffusive pow'r, 5
'Tis thine supreme, all substance to devour:
Æther, Sun, Moon, and Stars, light pure and clear,
For these thy lucid parts to men appear.
To thee, all dwellings, cities, tribes belong,
Diffus'd thro' mortal bodies bright and strong. 10
Hear, blessed power, to holy rites incline,
And all propitious on the incense shine:
Suppress the rage of fires unweary'd frame,
And still preserve our nature's vital flame.

Footnotes

*   This deity, according to Proclus, in Repub. p. 385. adorns by his artifice, the sensible machine of the universe, which he fills with certain reasons, proportions, and powers of Nature. But he requires the assistance of Venus, that he may invent sensible effects with beauty, and by this means cause the pulchritude of the world.

LXVI.

TO ESCULAPIUS.

The FUMIGATION from MANNA.

GREAT Esculapius, skill'd to heal mankind,
All-ruling Pæan, and physician kind;
Whose arts medic'nal, can alone assuage
Diseases dire, and stop their dreadful rage:
Strong lenient God, regard my suppliant pray'r,
Bring gentle Health, adorn'd with lovely hair;
Convey the means of mitigating pain,
And raging, deadly pestilence restrain.
O pow'r all-flourishing, abundant, bright,
Apollo's honor'd offspring, God of light; 10
Husband of blameless Health, the constant foe
Of dread Disease the minister of woe:

Come, blessed saviour, and my health defend,
And to my life afford a prosp'rous end.

LXVII.

TO HEALTH.

The FUMIGATION from MANNA.

O Much-desir'd, prolific, gen'ral queen,
Hear me, life-bearing, Health, of beauteous mien,
Mother of all; by thee diseases dire,
Of bliss destructive, from our life retire;
And ev'ry house is flourishing and fair, 5
If with rejoicing aspect thou art there:
Each dædal art, thy vig'rous force inspires,
And all the world thy helping hand desires;
Pluto life's bane alone resists thy will,
And ever hates thy all-preserving skill. 10
O fertile queen, from thee forever flows
To mortal life from agony repose;
And men without thy all-sustaining ease,
Find nothing useful, nothing form'd to please;
Without thy aid, not Plutus' self can thrive, 15
Nor man to much afflicted age arrive;
For thou alone of countenance serene,
Dost govern all things, universal queen.
Assist thy mystics with propitious mind,
And far avert disease of ev'ry kind.

LXVIII.

TO THE FURIES *

The FUMIGATION from AROMATICS.

VOCIFEROUS Bacchanalian Furies, hear!
Ye, I invoke, dread pow'rs, whom all revere;
Nightly, profound, in secret who retire,
Tisiphone, Alecto, and Megara dire:
Deep in a cavern merg'd, involv'd in night, 5
Near where Styx flows impervious to the sight;
Ever attendant on mysterious rites,
Furious and fierce, whom Fate's dread law delights;
Revenge and sorrows dire to you belong,
Hid in a savage veil, severe and strong, 10
Terrific virgins, who forever dwell
Endu'd with various forms, in deepest hell;
Aerial, and unseen by human kind,
And swiftly coursing, rapid as the mind.
In vain the Sun with wing'd refulgence bright, 15
In vain the Moon, far darting milder light,
Wisdom and Virtue may attempt in vain;
And pleasing, Art, our transport to obtain
Unless with these you readily conspire,
And far avert your all-destructive ire. 20

The boundless tribes of mortals you descry,
And justly rule with Right's impartial eye.
Come, snaky-hair'd, Fates many-form'd, divine,
Suppress your rage, and to our rites incline.

Footnotes

*   See the note to Hymn lviii. to the Fates.

LXIX.

TO THE FURIES.

The FUMIGATION from AROMATICS.

HEAR me, illustrious Furies, mighty nam'd,
Terrific pow'rs, for prudent counsel fam'd;
Holy and pure, from Jove terrestrial born
And Proserpine, whom lovely locks adorn:
Whose piercing sight, with vision unconfin'd, 5
Surveys the deeds of all the impious kind:
On Fate attendant, punishing the race
(With wrath severe) of deeds unjust and base.
Dark-colour'd queens, whose glittering eyes, are bright
With dreadful, radiant, life-destroying, light: 10
Eternal rulers, terrible and strong,
To whom revenge, and tortures dire belong;
Fatal and horrid to the human sight,
With snaky tresses wand'ring in the night;
Either approach, and in these rites rejoice, 15
For ye, I call, with holy, suppliant voice.

LXX.

TO MELINOE.

The FUMIGATION from AROMATICS.

Call Melinoe, saffron-veil'd, terrene,
Who from infernal Pluto's sacred queen,
Mixt with Saturnian Jupiter, arose,
Near where Cocytus' mournful river flows;
When under Pluto's semblance, Jove divine 5
Deceiv'd with guileful arts dark Proserpine.
Hence, Partly black thy limbs and partly white,
From Pluto dark, from Jove etherial, bright
Thy colour'd members, men by night inspire
When seen in specter'd forms with terrors dire; 10
Now darkly visible, involv'd in night,
Perspicuous now they meet the fearful fight.
Terrestrial queen expel wherever found
The soul's mad fears to earth's remotest bound;
With holy aspect on our incense shrine, 15
And bless thy mystics, and the rites divine.

LXXI.

TO FORTUNE.

The FUMIGATION from FRANKINCENSE.

Approach strong Fortune, with propitious mind
And rich abundance, to my pray'r inclin'd Placid,
and gentle Trivia, mighty nam'd, 3
Imperial Dian, born of Pluto fam'd;
Mankind's unconquer'd, endless praise is thine, 5
Sepulch'ral, widely-wand'ring pow'r divine!
In thee, our various mortal life is found,
And some from thee hi copious wealth abound;
While others mourn thy hand averse to bless,
In all the bitterness of deep distress. 10
Bc present, Goddess, to thy vot'ry kind,
And give abundance with benignant mind.

Footnotes

3   Ver. 3.] *Placid and gentle Trivia*. See the note to the Introduction to Musæus.

LXXII.

TO THE DÆMON, OR GENIUS.

The FUMIGATION from FRANKINCENSE.

THEE, mighty-ruling, Dæmon dread, I call,
Mild Jove, life-giving, and the source of all:
Great Jove, much-wand'ring, terrible and strong,
To whom revenge and tortures dire belong.
Mankind from thee, in plenteous wealth abound, 5
When in their dwellings joyful thou art found;
Or pass thro' life afflicted and distress'd,
The needful means of bliss by thee supprest.
'Tis thine alone endu'd with boundless might,
To keep the keys of sorrow and delight. 10

O holy, blessed father, hear my pray'r,
Disperse the seeds of life-consuming care;
With fav'ring mind the sacred rites attend,
And grant my days a glorious, blessed end.

LXXIII.

TO LEUCOTHEA.

The FUMIGATION from AROMATICS.

I Call Leucothea, of great Cadmus born,
And Bacchus' nurse, whom ivy leaves adorn.
Hear, pow'rful Goddess, in the mighty deep
Wide and profound, thy Ration doom'd to keep:
In waves rejoicing, guardian of mankind; 5
For ships from thee alone deliv'rance find
Amidst the fury of th' unstable main,
When art no more avail, and strength is vain;
When rushing billows with tempestuous ire
O'erwhelm the mariner in ruin dire, 10
Thou hear'st, with pity touch'd, his suppliant pray'r,
Resolv'd his life to succour and to spare.
Be ever present, Goddess! in distress,
Waft ships along with prosperous success:
Thy mystics thro' the stormy sea defend, 15
And safe conduct them to their destin'd end.

LXXIV.

TO PALÆMON.

The FUMIGATION from. MANNA.

O Nurs'd with Dionysius, doom'd to keep
Thy dwelling in the widely-spreading deep:
With joyful aspect to my pray'r incline,
Propitious come, and bless the rites divine:
Thro' earth and sea thy ministers attend, 5
And from old Ocean's stormy waves defend:
For ships their safety ever owe to thee,
Who wand'rest with them thro' the raging sea.
Come, guardian pow'r, whom mortal tribes desire,
And far avert the deep's destructive ire. 10

LXXV.

TO THE MUSES.

The FUMIGATION from FRANKINCENSE.

Daughters of Jove, dire-sounding and divine, [1]
Renown'd Pierian, sweetly speaking Nine;

To those whose breasts your sacred furies fire
Much-form'd, the objects of supreme desire:

Sources of blameless virtue to mankind, 5
Who form to excellence the youthful mind;

Who nurse the soul, and give her to descry
The paths of right with Reason's steady eye.

Commanding queens who lead to sacred light
The intellect refin'd from Error's night; 10

And to mankind each holy rite disclose,
For mystic knowledge from your nature flows.

Clio, and Erato, who charms the sight,
With thee Euterpe minist'ring delight:

Thalia flourishing, Polymina fam'd, 15
Melpomene from skill in music nam'd:

Terpischore, Urania heav'nly bright,
With thee * who gav'st me to behold the light.
Come, venerable, various, pow'rs divine,
With fav'ring aspect on your mystics shine; 20
Bring glorious, ardent, lovely, fam'd desire,
And warm my bosom with your sacred fire.

Footnotes

1   Ver. i.] *Daughters of Jove.* Proclus, in some manuscript commentary, cited by Gyraldus, in Syntag. de Musis. p.534. says that the Muses are called the daughters of Jove and Mnemosyne, because to those who desire to posses disciplines and sciences, intellect and the power of memory are necessary as the first requisites: the latter of which the Greeks call μνημονικὸσ, the former νοητικὸσ. But as the best explanation of the nature of the Muses is given by Proclus, in his Commentary or, Plato's Republic, p. 399. accompanied with all that philosophical elegance and subtilty which he possessed in so remarkable a degree, I persuade myself the following Paraphrase on his discourse concerning the different kinds of poets, will be highly acceptable to the liberal reader; and that its great excellence will amply compensate for its length.

"In the first place then, there are three poetic forms corresponding to the three different powers of the soul, Intellect, Reason, and Opinion. These we shall explain according to the opinion of Plato; and produce from Homer examples of each. The first kind of poetry then, is similar to intellect. But intellect is the best, most perfect, and most divine power of the soul: it is the most similar to a divine life, in the contemplation of which it is wholly employed, and is swallowed up as it were in the essence of divinity; so that it enkindles its own light from the splendor of the Gods, and conjoins its own most simple essence with supernatural unity. In like manner the most excellent kind of poetry, gives beatitude to the soul, from divinity, and places it among the Gods; participating by an ineffable union with the participated deities, and conjoining that which is filled with good, with its replenishing source. Hence it abstracts the soul from all material connections, illuminates it with celestial light, inflames it with a divine fire; and compels the whole inferior constitution of the soul, to be obedient to intellect alone. Indeed, a Fury of this kind is more excellent than any temperance; since it furnishes the soul with such a symmetry and proportion of divinity, that the very words bursting forth as its last effects, appear to be adorned with the beautiful bands of measure and number. For as prophetic fury arises from truth, and the amatorial from beauty; so the poetic proceeds from divine symmetry, by means of which it most intimately unites the poets with the Gods. Plato, in the Phædrus, speaking of this Fury, says that it is an occupation of the Muses; and a Fury sent from above on tender and untouched souls. That its employment is to fufcitate and inspire the poet, according to odes and the other kinds of poetry but its end, the instruction of posterity by celebrating the infinite deeds of antiquity. From these words it is plain, that Plato, in the first place, ascribes divinity to this kind of poetry, as being derived from the Muses; who fill as well intelligible as sensible works with paternal harmony, and ellegant motion. But he calls it an occupation, because the whole illustrated soul, resigns itself to the present effect of illuminating divinity: and a Fury, because it relinquishes its own proper ingenuity, and is carried according to the vigorous impulse of a superior power. Again, in the second place he describes the habit of the soul thus occupied: for, he say, it ought to be tender and untouched; not rigid, hard, and filled with many and various opinions, foreign from inspiring divinity: but it should be soft and tender, that it may easily admit divine inspiration; and untouched, that it may be sincere and empty of all other concerns. In the third place, he adds its common employment; that it is perfected by the afflatus of the Muses, and by the soul properly disposed for its reception. Indeed fafcitation is an elevation of the soul, an operation but little depraved, and a vigorous conversion to the deity, from a lapse into the whirls of generation. But an afflatus is a divine motion, and an unwearied musical dance towards the inspiring deity. Lastly, he testifies that human concerns spoken from a divine mouth, become more perfect, illustrious, and more convenient for the delivery of true doctrine to the hearers, Not that this kind of poetry is accommodated to juvenile tuition, but is the most convenient of all for the instruction of those who are perfect in politic discipline, and who earnestly desire the mystical tradition of divine concerns. On this account, Plato deservedly prefers it to all human arts. But he who (as he writes in the same place) approaches to the poetic gates, without the Fury of the Muses, trusting that he may become a good poet by a certain art, will be himself empty, as well as his poetry, in respect of that which proceeds from Fury; before whose presence, the poetry vanishes which is dictated by prudence alone." Thus far from the Phædrus.

Again, not dissimilar to these, are the words of Socrates in the Iö. For when the rhapsodist affirms, that he abounds with a copiousness of discourse on Homer, but not upon the other poets, Socrates ascribes the cause of this to his being moved by divine force, and not by art. For unless he was peculiarly inclined to Homer by a divine instinct, he would he equally as copious on all other poets as upon Homer. But the first mover says he is a God or a Muse, that is a divine cause; from thence the poet is excited, and from him again the rhapsodist. Hence poetic Fury is a medium between a divine principle and the rhapsodist, moving, and at the same time moved, and distributing supernal gifts to inferiors, by a certain latent consent; by means of which, these degrees cohere among themselves in the same manner as many iron rings depending from a magnet, each of which communicates in gradation, its alluring and attractive power to the other. So in the poetic chain, it is requisite there should be something divine, which, through proper mediums, may connect the last to the first monad. This Fury Homer, as well as Plato, calls at one time in the plural number Muses, and at another time in the singular number a Muse: in the first case, having respect to the multitude of the chain of the Muses; but in the second to the coherent union of all things, which is inserted from the first cause in inferior natures. For indeed poetry subsists in a secret and uniform manner in the first mover, and afterwards in poets excited by that unity, like the revolution of a thread from its bottom clew εἰνειλεγμένως, but in the rhapsodist's, according to the lowest and ministrant degree. And thus much it is sufficient for the present to have alledged from Plato's Iö. He who desires more, must consult that dialogue, where he will find many things commending this first and divine kind of Poets.

We shall farther add the testimony of the Athenian guest and of Timæus. For he exhorts us to follow poets seized with the Fury of Apollo, such being the sons of the Gods, and knowing in the best manner the concerns of their progenitors, although they deliver them without the assistance of arguments and demonstrations. And Plato, in the third book of his Laws, thus writes:

"This genus of poets is divine, it is agitated by the Gods, composes sacred hymns, and every where embraces Truth attended with the Graces and Muses." To which may be added, that in the first Alcibiades, he says, the nature of poetry is ænigmatical, and is not manifest to every understanding.

Indeed, you will find in Homer all kinds of poetry; but he has less of imagination and imitation, and excels in the first, concerning which we are now discoursing. For, inspired by the Muses and full of fury, he proposes mystical senses of divinity; such as concerning demiurgical unity, the triple division of the universe, the chains of Vulcan, and the connection of Jupiter with Juno. But Homer speaking of Demodocus (under whose person he wishes to signify himself, and on this account reports he was blind) says that he was a divine bard, loved by the Muses and their leader Apollo.

And thus much for the first kind of poets and poetry, according to Proclus; among which it is evident these Hymns must be ranked; as all sacred poetical composition belongs to this highest order. He then proceeds to the second kind of poetry, which the Greeks call διάνοια, or rational, as follows. Reason then is inferior to in dignity and power, yet it follows intellect as the leader of its energies, between which, and opinion, it is the connecting medium. And as soul by intellect is conjoined with the divinities; so by the assistance of reason it is converted into itself. Hence it revolves the multitude of arguments, considers the various differences of forms, collects intellect and the intelligent into one; and imitates in its operations an intelligible essence. But since prudence is the employment of reason, we attribute to it the second kind of poetry, which is a medium between the preceding, and the third which we shall next explain. This rational poetry, understands the essences of things, and is freely conversant about what is honest and good, as well in words as in actions, which are likewise the object of its contemplation. It produces every particular invested with elegant numbers and rythms; proposes moral sentences, the best counsels, intelligible moderation, and every virtue. Besides this, it teaches the circuits of the soul, its immortality and various powers; explains to mortals many names of an incorporeal nature, and produces many probable Dogmata respecting corporeal substance. The Athenian guest (in Plato, lib. i. De Legibus) testifies, that the poetry of Theognis is of this kind, which, because it teaches and commends every virtue, is justly to be preferred to the poetry of Tyrtæus, which exhorts to fortitude alone. But Homer represents this species of poetry, when he describes the life of the soul, the different essences of her parts, the difference between the image and the usurping soul, the variety subsisting in nature, the order of the elements of the universe, civil offices, and the like. But Homer himself, appears to have made Phemius the lyrist skilled in this kind of poetry, where Penelope says to him, lib. i.

"Alluring arts thou know'st, and what of old
"Of Gods and heroes, sacred bards have told."

After the two superior kinds of poetry, that inspired by Fury, and the rational; it remains to speak of the imitative. This last kind of poetry, then, is far distant from the excellence of the others; since it employs imaginations, opinions, and the irrational senses; from whence it contracts many vices, especially in that part of it, which is called phantastic. For it greatly raises moderate affection, disturbs the hearers, and, together with words, various harmonies, and numbers, changes the affections of the soul. It shadows over the nature of things not such as they are, but such as they appear to vulgar inspection; and explains them not according to an exact knowledge, but from a delusive imagination. Besides this, it proposes as its end the delight of its auditors; and particularly regards that part of the soul, which is obnoxious to the passions of joy and grief. But it is subdivided into two other kinds, one of which is conjectural or assimilatory, and the other phantastic. The latter of these represents only the apparent imitation and similitude, not that which is true; and considers its end accomplished, if it produces in the hearers pleasure and delight, belonging to the phantasy alone. But the other does not so much study the gratification of the popular ear, as a proper imitation, that it may express the things themselves, and exhibit to the eyes an exquisite image of that, concerning which it treats, and may as near as possible, express the exemplars which it imitates. But Plato himself, under the person of the Eleatean guest (in Sophista) describes the differences of each of these as follows. "I now appear to discern two species of imitation, one conjectural, or the art of assimilating, whose business is to fabricate an image emulous of its exemplar, as far as pertains to length, breadth, depth, and convenient colours. Theæt. Do not those who imitate something, perform this to the utmost of their ability? Guest. Not those who fashion or paint any great work. For if they bestowed on the resemblances the true commensuration of beautiful things, the superior members would appear less than is proper, and the inferior larger: because the one is beheld by us at a distance, the other near at hand. Theæt. Intirely so. Guest. Hence artists neglecting truth, do not accommodate to resemblances such commensurations as are really beautiful, but only such as appear so." From these words it is plain that Plato distinguishes each kind of imitation, not only in painting and statuary, but also in poetry; which he compares with those imitative arts. Again, the Athenian guest speaks separately of the conjectural kind, where he treats of that music which does not propose to itself pleasure, but a true and most similar imitation of its exemplar, as in the second book of Laws. Indeed, Socrates speaks of the phantastic kind in the tenth book of the Republic, comparing it to a picture which does not represent the works of nature, but of artists; and these not such as they are, but such as they appear, not imitating their reality, but only their phantastic representation. He likewise demonstrates that this kind of poetry is phantastic and is in the third degree from truth. But each kind of imitation is found in Homer. For he is then to be esteemed phantastic when he affirms any thing according to vulgar opinion; such as when ascribing the rising and setting of the sun, not from true situations, but from such as appear so to the senses, which are deceived by distance of place, But where he preserves types of imitation convenient to persons and things, as when he imitates heroes fighting, consulting, and speaking, framing deeds and discourses adapted to the life and pursuits of each, he ought to be called a conjectural poet. And of this kind perhaps is the lyrist of Clytemnestra, who so learnedly imitated examples of temperance by right opinion, that Clytemnestra was free from fault, while he resided with her. But it is lawful to call the musician Thamyris, phantastic, who, instead of the ancient and simple music, endeavoured to introduce one more pleasant, diversified in many ways, and calculated to please the senses and the vulgar. Hence he is feigned to have contended with the Muses themselves, by whom, having raised their anger, he was blinded; not that in reality the Muses are affected with anger, but because he was incapable of the true, simple, and ancient music; and laboured only to move the affectons and imagination, not following right opinion, or the science of imitation.

* Calliope.

LXXVI.

To MNEMOSYNE, or the GODDESS of MEMORY *.

The FUMIGATION from FRANKINCENSE.

THE consort I invoke of Jove divine,
Source of the holy, sweetly-speaking Nine;

Free from th' oblivion of the fallen mind,
By whom the soul with intellect is join'd:
Reason's increase, and thought to thee belong, 5
All-powerful, pleasant, vigilant, and strong:
'Tis thine, to waken from lethargic rest
All thoughts deposited within the breast;
And nought neglecting, vigorous to excite
The mental eye from dark oblivion's night. 10
Come, blessed power, thy mystic's mem'ry wake
To holy rites, and Lethe's fetters break.

Footnotes

* Memory, according to the Platonic philosophy, is that power by which the soul is enabled to profer in some future period, some former energy: and the energy of this power is reminiscence. Now the very essence of intellect is energy, and all its perceptions are nothing more than visions of itself: but all the energies of soul are derived from intellectual illumination. Hence we may compare intellect to light, the soul to an eye, and Memory to that power by which the soul is converted to the light, and actually perceives. But the visions of the soul participate of greater or less reality, in proportion as she is more or less intimately converted to the divine light of intellect. In the multitude of mankind, indeed, the eye of the soul perceives with but a glimmering light, being accustomed to look constantly abroad into the dark and fluctuating regions of sense, and to contemplate solely the shadowy forms of imagination; in consequence of which, their memory is solely employed on objects obscure, external, and low. But in the few who have purified that organ of the soul, by which truth can alone be perceived, and which, as Plato says, is better worth saving than ten thousand eyes of sense; who have disengaged this eye from that barbaric clay with which it was buried, and have by this means turned it as from some benighted day, to bright and real vision: in these, Souls, Memory, and Reminiscense, are entirely conversant with those divine ideal forms, so familiar to the soul before her immersion in body. Hence, since we were formerly intellectual natures, we ought, as Porphyry observes, not only to think earnestly of the way, however long and laborious, by which we may return to things truly our own; but that we may meet with a more favourable reception from our proper kindred, we should meditate in what manner we may divest ourselves of every thing foreign from our true country, and recall to our memory those dispositions and habits, without which, we cannot be admitted by our own, and which from long disuse, have departed from our souls. For this purpose (says he) we must lay aside whatever we have associated to ourselves from a mortal nature; and hasten our return to the contemplation of the simple and immutable light of good. We must divest ourselves of the various garments of mortality, by which our true beauty is concealed; and enter the place of contest naked, and without the incumbrance of dress, striving for the most glorious of all prizes, the Olympiad of the soul. Thus far Porphyry: and thus it appears, that the poet, with great philosophical propriety, celebrates Memory as uniting the soul with intellect.

LXXVII.

TO AURORA.

The FUMIGATION from MANNA.

HEAR me, O Goddess! whose emerging ray
Leads on the broad refulgence of the day;
Blushing Aurora, whose celestial light
Beams on the world with red'ning splendours bright:
Angel of Titan, whom with constant round, 5
Thy orient beams recall from night profound:
Labour of ev'ry kind to lead is thine,
Of mortal life the minister divine.
Mankind in thee eternally delight,
And none presumes to shun thy beauteous sight. 10
Soon as thy splendours break the bands of rest,
And eyes unclose with pleasing sleep oppress'd;
Men, reptiles, birds, and beasts, with gen'ral voice,
And all the nations of the deep, rejoice;
For all the culture of our life is thine. 15
Come, blessed pow'r! and to these rites incline:
Thy holy light increase, and unconfin'd
Diffuse its radiance on thy mystic's mind.

LXXVIII.

TO THEMIS.

The FUMIGATION from FRANKINCENSE.

ILLUSTRIOUS Themis, of celestial birth,
Thee I invoke, young blossom of the earth; [2]
Beauteous-eyed virgin; first from thee alone,
Prophetic oracles to men were known,
Giv'n from the deep recesses of the fane 5
In sacred Pytho, where renown'd you reign;
From thee, Apollo's oracles arose,
And from thy pow'r his inspiration flows.
Honour'd by all, of form divinely bright,
Majestic virgin, wand'ring in the night: 10
Mankind from thee first learnt initial rites,
And Bacchus' nightly choirs thy soul delights;
For holy honours to disclose is thine,
With all the culture of the pow'rs divine.
Be present, Goddess, to my pray'r inclin'd,
And bless the mystic rites with fav'ring mind.

Footnotes

2   Ver. 2.] *Young blossom of the earth.* See the note to Hymn xi, to Hercules.

LXXIX.

TO THE NORTH WIND.

The FUMIGATION from FRANKINCENSE.

BOREAS, whose wint'ry blasts, terrific, tear
The bosom of the deep surrounding air;
Cold icy pow'r, approach, and fav'ring blow,
And Thrace a while desert expos'd to snow:
The misty station of the air dissolve, 5
With pregnant clouds, whose frames in show'rs resolve:
Serenely temper all within the sky,
And wipe from moisture, Æther's beauteous eye.

LXXX.

TO THE WEST WIND.

The FUMIGATION from FRANKINCENSE.

SEA-born, aerial, blowing from the west,
Sweet gales, who give to weary'd labour rest:
Vernal and grassy, and of gentle found,
To ships delightful, thro' the sea profound;
For these, impell'd by you with gentle force, 5
Pursue with prosp'rous Fate their destin'd course.
With blameless gales regard my suppliant pray'r,
Zephyrs unseen, light-wing'd, and form'd from air.

LXXXI.

TO THE SOUTH WIND.

The FUMIGATION from FRANKINCENSE.

WIDE coursing gales, whose lightly leaping feet
With rapid wings the air's wet bosom beat,
Approach benevolent, swift-whirling pow'rs,
With humid clouds the principles of flow'rs:
For flow'ry clouds are portion'd to your care, 5
To send on earth from all surrounding air.
Bear, blessed pow'rs, these holy rites attend,
And fruitful rains on earth all-parent send.

LXXXII.

TO OCEAN.

The Fumigation from AROMATICS

OCEAN I call, whose nature ever flows,
From whom at first both Gods and men arose;
Sire incorruptible, whose waves surround, 3
And earth's concluding mighty circle bound:

Hence every river, hence the spreading sea, 5
And earth's pure bubbling fountains spring from thee:
Hear, mighty fire, for boundless bliss is thine,
Whose waters purify the pow'rs divine:
Earth's friendly limit, fountain of the pole,
Whose waves wide spreading and circumfluent roll.
Approach benevolent, with placid mind,
And be for ever to thy mystics kind.

Footnotes

3   LXXXII. Ver. 3.] *Whose waves surround*, &c. Gesner well observes, that this opinion of the ocean surrounding the earth, is exceeding ancient. see his Præl. i. de Navigationibus vet. § I.

LXXXIII.

TO VESTA.

The FUMIGATION from AROMATICS.

Daughter of Saturn, venerable dame,
The seat containing of unweary'd flame; 2

In sacred rites these ministers are thine,
Mystics much-blessed, holy and divine
In thee, the Gods have fix'd place, 5
Strong, stable, basis of the mortal race:
Eternal, much-form'd ever-florid queen,
Laughing and blessed, and of lovely mien; 8

Accept these rites, accord each just desire,
And gentle health, and needful good inspire.

Footnotes

2 XXXIII. Ver. 2] *The seat containing of unweary'd flame.* Vesta is celebrated in this Hymn as the earth, and is the same with the mother of the Gods; as is evident from the Hymn to that divinity, in which she is expressly called Vesta. Now this perfectly agrees with the fragment of Philolaus the Pythagorean, preserved by Stobæus, in Eclog. Phys. p. 51. "Philolaus (says he) places fire in

the middle at the centre, which he calls the Vesta of the universe, the house of Jupiter, the mother of the Gods, and the basis, coherence, and measure of nature." From whence it appears, that they are greatly mistaken who suppose the Pythagoreans meant the sun, by the fire at the centre: and this is still more evident, from the following words of Simplicius de Cælo, lib ii. Οἱ δὲ γνησίςερον ἀυτον μετασχόντες, μετασχόντες, τὸ μὲν πῦρ ἐν τῷ μέσῳ φασὶ τὴν δημιυργικην δίναμιν, εκ τῦ μέσυ ὅλην τηγ γην τρέφυσαν, καὶ τὸ ψυχόμενον ἀυτῆς ἀνεγέιρυσαν. δἰ ὃ οἱ μέν, ΖΗΝΟΣ ΠΥΡΓΟΝ ἀυτὸ καλυσιν. ὡσ ἀυτὸς ἐν τοῖσ Πυθαγορείοις διηγήσατο. οἱ δὲ ΔΙΟΣ ΦΥΛΑΚΗΝ ὡσ ἐν τύτοις. οἳ δὲ, ΔΙΟΣ ΘΡΟΝΟΝ᾽ ὡς ἄλλοι φασίν. χεδνρον (sic lege et non ἄντρον) δὲ τὴν γῆν ἔλεγον, ὡς ὄργανον καὶ αὐτὴν τῦ χρονῦ ἡμερων γαρ ἐςιν ἄυτη, καὶ νυχτων, αἰτία. That is, "But those who more clearly perceive these affairs, call the fire in the middle a demiurgic power, nourishing the whole earth from the midst, and exciting and enlivening whatever it contains of a frigid nature: on which account some call it the tower of Jupiter, as he (i.e. Aristotle) relates in his Phythagorics. But others, the keeper or guardian of Jove; as he relates in these (i.e. his books of Cælo). But according to others, it is the throne of Jupiter. But they called the earth a centre, as being itself an organ or instrument of time: for it is the cause of day and night."

8 Ver. 8] *Laughing and blessed.* Proclus, in Plat. Rep. p. 384. observes, that we ought to interpret the laughter of the Gods as an exuberant operation in the universe; and the gladness of mundane concerns, under the providence of a divine cause. But since such a providence, says he, is incomprehensible, and is a never failing communication of all divine goods; we must allow that Homer justly calls the laughter of the Gods ἄσβεςος {Greek *á?sbesos*} or inextinguishable. He adds, that fables do not represent the Gods as always weeping, but affirm that they laugh without ceasing; because tears are symbols of their providence in mortal concerns, which are continually subject to existence and decay: but laughter is a sign of their effects in the universe, and of its principal parts, which are ever moved in one and the same orderly manner. Hence, since we divide demiurgical powers between Gods and men, we assign laughter to the generation of the Gods, but tears to the formation of men or animals. Hence, the poet sings in his Hymn to the Sun, *O Apollo, the mortal race of men is the subject of thy tears; but the celestial race of Gods springs from laughter.* But since we divide the works of divinity into things celestial, and those subject to the moon; after the same manner, we

attribute laughter to the first, and grief to the second. Lastly, when we reason concerning the generations and corruptions of things below the moon, we refer the one to the weeping, and the other to the laughter of the Gods. And hence in our mysteries, the ministers of sacred rites, at a certain time order each of these to be celebrated. He then concludes with *an excellent observation*, that men of simple understandings are unable to comprehend intellectually mystical ceremonies and fables of this kind; since *such men* destitute of science, produce nothing but absurd confusion about the religion of the Gods.

LXXXIV.

TO SLEEP.

The FUMIGATION from a Poppy.

SLEEP, king of Gods, and men of mortal birth,
Sov'reign of all sustain'd by mother Earth;

For thy dominion is supreme alone,
O'er all extended, and by all things known.
'Tis thine all bodies with benignant mind 5
In other bands than those of brass to bind:
Tamer of cares, to weary toil repose,
From whom sweet solace in affliction flows.
Thy pleasing, gentle chains preserve the soul,
And e'en the dreadful cares of death controul; 10
For death and Lethe with oblivious stream,
Mankind thy genuine brothers justly deem.
With fav'ring aspect to my pray'r incline,
And save thy mystics in their works divine.

LXXXV.

TO THE DIVINITY OF DREAMS.

The FUMIGATION from AROMATICS.

THEE I invoke, blest pow'r of dreams divine,
Angel of future fates, swift wings are thine:
Great source of oracles to human kind,
When stealing soft, and whisp'ring to the mind,
Thro' sleep's sweet silence and the gloom of night, 5
Thy pow'r awakes th' intellectual fight;
To silent souls the will of heav'n relates,
And silently reveals their future fates.
For ever friendly to the upright mind
Sacred and pure, to holy rites inclin'd; 10

For these with pleasing hope thy dreams inspire,
Bliss to anticipate, which all desire.
Thy visions manifest of fate disclose,
What methods best may mitigate our woes;
Reveal what rites the Gods immortal please, 15
And what the means their anger to appease:
For ever tranquil is the good man's end,
Whose life, thy dreams admonish and defend.

But from the wicked turn'd averse to bless,
Thy form unseen, the angel of distress; 20
No means to cheek approaching ill they find,
Pensive with fears, and to the future blind.
Come, blessed pow'r, the signatures reveal
Which heav'n's decrees mysteriously conceal,
Signs only present to the worthy mind, 25
Nor omens ill disclose of monst'rous kind.

LXXXVI.

TO DEATH.

The FUMIGATION from MANNA.

HEAR me, O Death, whose empire unconfin'd,
Extends to mortal tribes of ev'ry kind.
On thee, the portion of our time depends,
Whose absence lengthens life, whose presence ends.

Thy sleep perpetual bursts the vivid folds, 5
By which the soul, attracting body holds: 6

Common to all of ev'ry sex and age,
For nought escapes thy all-destructive rage;

Not youth itself thy clemency can gain,
Vig'rous and strong, by thee untimely slain. 10
In thee, the end of nature's works is known,
In thee, all judgment is absolv'd alone:
No suppliant arts thy dreadful rage controul,
No vows revoke the purpose of thy soul;

O blessed pow'r regard my ardent pray'r, 15
And human life to age abundant spare.

THE END.

Footnotes

6 Ver. 6.] *By which the soul*, &c. This is best explained by Porphyry in his excellent work entitled Ἀφορμαὶ πεὸσ τὰ Νοητά 8. as follows: "Whatever nature binds, nature again dissolves; and that which the soul conciliates into union, the soul disperses and dissolves. Nature, indeed, bound the body to the soul; but the soul ties herself to the body. Hence, nature frees the body from the soul, but the soul by the exercise of philosophy, separates herself from the deadly bands of the body." And again, in the next sentence, "Death is of two kinds, the one equally known to all men, when the body is separated from the soul; but the other peculiar to philosophers, when the soul is separated from the body: nor does the one always attend the other." Now this two-fold death we must understand in the following manner: that though some particular body may be loosened from the soul, yet while material passions and affections reside in the soul, the soul will continually verge to another body, and as long as this inclination continues, remain connected with the body. But when from the dominion of an intellectual nature, the soul is separated from material affections, it is truly liberated from the body; though the body at the same time verges and clings to the soul, as to the immediate cause of its support. And thus much for a Commentary on the Hymns or Initiations of Orpheus. But before I conclude the present work, I beg leave to address a few words to the liberal and philosophical part of my readers. You then, as the votaries of truth, will, I doubt not, unite with me in most earnest wishes, that every valuable work on the Platonic philosophy was well translated into our native tongue; that we might no longer be subject to the toil of learning the ancient languages. The mischief, indeed, resulting from the study of words is almost too apparent to need any illustration; as the understanding is generally contra its vigour exhausted; and the genius fettered to verbal criticism, and grammatical trifles. Hence an opinion is gradually formed, that the Greek philosophy can alone be understood in the Greek tongue: and thus the books

containing the wisdom of antiquity, are for the most part deposited, in the hands of men, incapable of comprehending their contents. While an opinion so sordid prevails, amidst all our refinements in arts, and increasing mass of experiments, we must remain with respect to philosophy in a state of barbarous ignorance. We may flourish, indeed, as a commercial people; and stretch the rod of empire over nations as yet unknown. The waters of Thames, heavy laden with the wealth of merchandize, and sonorous with the din of trade, may devolve abundance in a golden tide; but we must remember that the Dæmon of commerce is at the same time advancing with giant strides, to trample on the most liberal pursuits, and is preparing with his extended savage arm, to crush the votaries of truth, and depopulate the divine retreats of philosophy. Rise then ye liberal few, and vindicate the dignity of ancient wisdom. Bring truth from her silent and sacred concealments, and vigorously repel the growing empire of barbaric taste; which bids fair to extinguish the celestial fire of philosophy in the rigid embraces of philology, and to bury the divine light of mind, in the sordid gloom of sense. But if your labours should prove abortive; if the period is yet at a distance, when truth shall once more establish her kingdom; when another dream like that of Ilissus, shall become tuneful with the music of philosophy; and other cities like those of Athens and Alexandria, be filled with the sacred haunts of philosophers: there yet remains an inheritance for the lovers of wisdom in the regions of intellect, those fortunate islands of truth, where all is tranquil and serene, beyond the of power of chance, and the reach of change. Let us then fly from hence my friends, to those delightful realms: for there, while connected with body, we may find a retreat from the storms and tempests of a corporeal life. Let us build for ourselves the raft of virtue, and departing from this region of sense, like Ulysses from the charms of Calypso, direct our course by the light of ideas, those bright intellectual stars, through the dark ocean of a material nature, until we arrive at our father's land. For there having divested ourselves of the torn garments of mortality, as much as our union with body will permit, we may resume our natural appearance; and may each of us at length, recover the ruined empire of his soul.

BIBLIOBAZAAR

The essential book market!

Did you know that you can get any of our titles in large print?

Did you know that we have an ever-growing collection of books in many languages?

**Order online:
www.bibliobazaar.com**

Find all of your favorite classic books!

Stay up to date with the latest government reports!

At BiblioBazaar, we aim to make knowledge more accessible by making thousands of titles available to you- *quickly and affordably*.

Contact us:
BiblioBazaar
PO Box 21206
Charleston, SC 29413

CPSIA information can be obtained at www.ICGtesting.com
Printed in the USA
LVOW10s1401301114

416285LV00031B/967/A

9 780559 071577